THE VIRGIN INTERNET
MUSIC GUIDE

THE VIRGIN INTERNET MUSIC GUIDE

VERSION 1.0

by Dominic Wills
and Ben Wardle

In association with

CLICKMUSIC.co.uk

This edition first published in 2000 by
Virgin Publishing Ltd
Thames Wharf Studios
Rainville Road
London
W6 9HA

First published in Great Britain in 2000 by Virgin Publishing Ltd

Version 1.0 – May 2000

A catalogue record for this book is available from the British Library.

ISBN 0 7535 0446 4

Designed and typeset by John and Orna Designs, London
Printed and bound by Caledonian International
Book Manufacturers Ltd

//LOOKING FOR MUSIC ON THE INTERNET? HOLD ON TO YOUR HATS

Ten years ago, few of us would have imagined that revolution was just around the corner. Despite a slew of books and films stretching back to HG Wells, Jules Verne and beyond, telling us over and over that scientific advancement might see men achieve the easy life, how could we have known that we were about to witness a step forward that would hand us vital and hitherto hidden information, and allow us to organise our lives and cheaply purchase all we need without ever leaving the house?

Today, thanks to the Internet, we can buy our plane tickets, book our hotels, find suitable pets, vote for our politicians, buy our weekly groceries and (maybe) discover the truth behind the JFK assassination. We can also, by building our own website, or contributing to the thousands of newsgroups and millions of chat rooms and message boards, say anything we like. This is a major liberation that anyone with access to a linked-up computer can enjoy.

And music fits perfectly into this brave new world. New technology is making it easier and easier to transfer music and video over the Internet, directly into our homes. Our computer is beginning to take the place of our radio, television and stereo system, all at once. Digital storage allows us to collect thousands of albums, without having to move into a bigger apartment. Record companies and CD retailers are using the Internet to make millions of songs available that would otherwise have been lost for ever. And the competition is so intense that prices are falling on a daily basis. There's never been a better time to love music.

Beyond the actual purchasing of singles and albums (though the Internet means you no longer have to buy one or the other: you can have whichever tracks you like), the availability of everything musical is changing. Just as you can buy a car over the Internet and have it delivered, so you can obtain instruments, equipment, sheet music, books, anything. You can find out about all of the musical events taking place in your area and worldwide, and buy tickets for them. If you can't make it to the gig, no worries. More and more of them are being broadcast over the Internet anyway.

The Internet is a fantastic boon if you're a musician, too. Here you can find detailed directories of studios, producers, mixers, equipment, venues, everything. Unbelievably, you can make your music available to everyone without the aid of record companies, and receive feedback direct from your fans. And it's also possible that everyone in the world could own a copy of your record without your ever having received a penny. What a bummer!

On the Internet, particularly in the incredibly fast-paced music market, things are changing so quickly that even the experts are having a hard time keeping up. It's known as the Wild West for good reason. There are millions of sites competing for your attention, and millions more appearing as short months go by. Many are brilliantly entertaining, conceived and executed by people who really ought to be working with George Lucas or Steven Spielberg. Many – as you'd expect in an industry where performers can be pelted with wet panties, or even stalked and shot – are obsessive and all the more fascinating for that. And many are, of course, tedious nonsense, put together by the untalented and uninspired.

This guide is not here to give you the basics of the Internet. For that, you need **The Virgin Guide to the Internet**. What you'll find here is clear information – for scholars, fans and bands alike – on how to make the best of music on the Internet, as well as thousands of addresses for the best sites in existence. There's something (a lot, actually) for fans of rock, reggae, pop, nostalgia, indie, rap, classical, jazz, folk, R&B – you name it. Try them out, then do the thing that makes the Internet such a blast – surf. Follow the links to the rainbow's end, or at least until your phone bill gets too scary.

Above all, enjoy.

//ABOUT CLICKMUSIC

With literally millions of websites dedicated to music on the net, Clickmusic.co.uk makes sense of the noise by helping to sort the good from the bad.

The Clickmusic search facility takes you to the best, whether you're looking for MP3s, local gig listings, album reviews or simply searching for an artist. Clickmusic provides music fans with the most up-to-the-minute source for music news and reviews, updating breaking news stories every five minutes every day. And if you're buying CDs, sheet music, hi-fi hardware, MP3 players or musical instruments online, Clickmusic brings you the largest selection of online retailers in one place.

//ABOUT THE AUTHORS

Dominic Wills is a music journalist. Working first for *Melody Maker*, then *Uncut*, the *Guardian* and the *Sunday Times*, he now works extensively for film and music magazines on the Internet. Virgin have also published his most excellent biography of the Charlatans.

Ben Wardle has worked as an A&R man for various major record companies, signing a wide variety of bands, some of whom appeared on television and sold records. Now Music Editor at Clickmusic, he fritters away the spare time he has left on his indie label Scared Hitless.

//CONTENTS

9//WE WANT IT ALL, WE WANT IT ALL ... 185

and we want it now. Essential advice for musicians and bands.

10//THE FUTURE NOW? 219

What's around the corner, or at least what we think might be.

1// THE REVOLUTION IS HERE

From the beginning of the last century, with its itinerant blues men, through the crazy years of jazz and on to today, music has always seemed to find itself right at the cutting edge of cultural change. Think Elvis, and the riots around Bill Haley. Think Flower Power in the San Francisco of 1965. Think of the Beatles and the Stones, of Johnny Rotten, Kurt Cobain and Acid House. Revolution and massive innovation always seems to have its very own soundtrack.

Today the biggest changes in our lives are, it seems, being wrought by the increasing popularity of the Internet. What began in 1964 as an effort to protect the fledgling US military computer network – connecting a number of separate computers, each of which would share the same information, would mean that one nuclear bomb could not disable the whole system – has far outgrown its original concept. What was intended to be the connection of just a few computers has come to connect millions of them.

Basically, information is stored on servers, which can be anything from a simple PC to a high-powered tower. These are just computers that sit waiting for requests for information, which they supply on demand. Via an ISP (an Internet Service Provider, such as AOL or Virgin Net), you connect your computer to one of these servers, and can then connect to any of the millions of servers on the Internet and discover what information they hold. To acquaint yourself with the basics of the Internet, its history and many of the delights it can offer, check out the excellent **The Virgin Guide to the Internet**.

Since 1991, when it was opened up to the public and commercial organisations, the Internet has quickly come to touch many aspects of our lives. Many of us now shop in virtual supermarkets, choosing our goods over the Net, paying by card, and having them delivered next day. We use the Internet to plan our holidays, to buy our plane and train tickets. We can virtually check out the best schools for our children, we can bank online. We can buy a car, and even a house. We can watch sporting events and movies. Some people will set up camera systems allowing us to see into their bedroom 24 hours a day. If we didn't have to exercise and socialise, many of us have no real reason to leave our homes. It's incredible.

And, of course, whenever things are incredible, music is there. There are some who'll claim that contemporary music – pulsing, bleeping, thrilling dance music – is the perfect soundtrack for a technological revolution, just as the Stones' 'Street Fighting Man' was appropriate to Europe 1968 with its widespread student unrest. And they do have a point. But music's main relevance comes from its very own nature. Even when it isn't recorded digitally (as almost all music is these days), it's easily digitised. You'll perhaps recall the CD revolution, when the record companies persuaded everyone to purchase all their favourite albums again on the grounds that on the new format they were 'digitally remastered'? Well, that's kind of happening again.

Music, like any information, is easily broken down into zeroes and ones, and is consequently well suited to being transferred through the cables and phone lines that connect us to the Internet. On top of this, there's been other great technological advancements allowing music files to be effectively 'compressed' – made smaller without any loss of sound quality, so that music can be transferred – ever more rapidly.

So people can send music fairly easily across the Internet, but why would they? After all, most would see it as a luxury item. With all the sensitive, potentially life-changing political information out there, and all the activists ready and willing to pump it into our homes, you'd think music would be placed on the back burner for some considerable time yet. But the fact is that music is actually a vital part of our lives – we all love it, in some shape or form.

And, besides, the music industry is now worth some $40 billion a year. The combination of music's ease of transfer over the Net and the rapid change in our purchasing habits is more than most venture capitalists can bear. Billions have been spent in the last couple of years as companies have battled for domination of this new and immensely lucrative market, each of them putting their massive resources into the perfection of software and hardware. And these billions – by financing the discovery and testing of new formats for storing, ordering and transferring musical information, and secure ways of purchasing – have powered the advance of the Internet itself.

The big change and what you need to keep up
In the following chapters we'll see what changes the Internet has brought about in the music industry. We'll see how record companies have been forced to reassess (or not) their relationships with artists, retailers and customers, how they're struggling with pirates and freedom fighters to keep control over the distribution of music, and how their troubles are bringing about benefits for music fans the world over.

We'll also see how retailers are adapting to this sea change in an already volatile market, and consequently how the Internet helps us find more brilliant music – more quickly and cheaply than ever before. We'll see how magazines are coping and changing, how they're suddenly free to play to their strengths and can therefore provide us with the best service ever. We'll see how bands can use the Internet to advance their careers, in both a new and traditional sense. We'll see the best and worst sites on offer from fans and bands alike, and we'll look at the best guides to show us around the web.

Oh, and we're going to take a close look at the notorious MP3 format. You've surely heard of it – it's the format that apparently frees us from ever having to pay for music again. Hold on to your hats.

In order to sample the musical wares on offer – and there is an enormous number of samples to be tested, and even freebies to be had – you'll need to have the right equipment. This is important as many music sites allow you to download not only music, but also the software to store, order and play it. They also like to use the latest in Flash technology, with all manner of chaotic animation, and they like to drop 'cookies' on to your hard disk, so they can keep tabs on your likes and dislikes whenever you visit them (a cookie is a scrap of information that a website creates on your computer's hard disk). You need to be prepared, Mr Baden-Powell.

Have no fear on the equipment front. Most new computers will be fine, as will many, many older ones. If you have an IBM-compatible PC, you'll want the very latest version of Windows preinstalled and a nippy processor running at at least 250MHz (Intel's latest Pentium would be good). Sixty-four megabytes of RAM (main memory) would be helpful, though you could make do with 32. Go for a fast modem, with a transfer rate of 56kbps, and the fastest CD-ROM drive you can get, making sure it's ready for DVD. You'll also be wanting a sound card – 16-bit at the very least – and decent speakers. Then you'll need a monitor and graphics adapter. The majority of web pages are intended to be displayed at a resolution of 800 x 600 – go higher.

For those of you with Macintosh, you'll be needing System 8. You'll need 64Mb of RAM; the hard disk needs a good 4-6Gb capacity; and you too will want a resolution of at least 800 x 600 from your monitor and graphics adapter, with 256 colours.

Whatever system you're using, make sure you're running a decent browser. You'll need Microsoft's Internet Explorer at 4.01 – later is better – or Netscape Navigator at 4.05. Again, go later if you can. In fact, make sure everything is as powerful as you can make it. There can be no doubt that you'll be updating far more quickly than you imagine.

Accept the system and get what you need
Extreme competition between companies battling to popularise their software and hardware means that you'll find excellent music being made available for download in an increasing number of formats. The main ones for now are MP3, Liquid Audio, and RealAudio, though Microsoft is currently on the warpath with its Windows Media format, doing deals with major players like Yahoo!

Let's consider RealAudio first, and to do that we must first consider the concept of 'streaming'. Most users really don't have sufficiently fast Internet access to quickly download multimedia files of the size we see today. Albums and videos are made up of a lot of information, after all. Streaming, a technique whereby data is transferred in such a way that it can be processed as a smooth and continuous stream, allows the client's browser or plug-in to actually start displaying (or playing) the data before the entire file has been transmitted.

RealAudio (http://www.real.com), the first site to allow users to download and run audio clips in real time, is the 'de facto standard' for streaming and, developed by RealNetworks (formerly Progressive Networks), it supports FM-stereo quality sound. Owing to RealNetworks' constant updating and improving of their players – RealPlayer and the fantastic RealJukebox – RealAudio has continued to dominate. When gigs or interviews are broadcast live on the Net, or when record companies and Internet shops make tracks and clips of tracks available for you to sample, it's often done in RealAudio.

So you'll need a RealPlayer which, unsurprisingly given all that competition, is not only freely available for download wherever there's a RealAudio sound file to be played, but also included in current versions of both Netscape Navigator and Microsoft Internet Explorer. If you wish, you can purchase the latest model, the RealPlayer 7 Plus, at Real.com for a mere $29.99 – the price at the time of writing – including 36 albums in RealAudio, among them offerings by Foo Fighters, Toni Braxton and Sarah McLachlan.

But RealAudio is the nice side of music on the Internet. No one has a bad word to say about it. That's amazing, considering the ferocious struggle for control over digital downloading that's still raging. The deals now being done between the software companies, servers and search engines will change the face of music on the Internet. They'll decide what and how you download, and how much you pay. Best to know the various combatants then ...

Digital downloading and the redistribution of distribution

It's been predicted that, by the year 2002, digital music sales will be bringing in around $30 million per annum – not a big slice of the $40 billion made yearly by the music industry. The major record companies, though, fear that this might be a foolish estimate. As cable modems and digital subscriber lines (DSL and ADSL) become widely available outside the United States, allowing customers to download tracks in seconds rather than painfully frustrating minutes, the market may expand furiously.

Our purchasing habits are changing drastically. It's reckoned that over 20 per cent of American Net users have already bought CDs over the Net, and the percentage is increasing. Might they not be just as prepared to download music direct on to their computer, if its sound system were of adequate quality? Wouldn't they prefer to pick out their own favourite tracks from vast lists and 'burn' their own CDs, with their own sleeve designs? And what if people started to make music available for nothing? It seemed possible, with digital technology, that one single person could get hold of an artist's music, copy it, upload it to the Internet and thereby allow millions to make their own copy, with no loss of sound quality whatsoever.

The MP3 format, whereby the sounds on a CD are compressed and made more suitable for transfer across the Internet, caused a terrible headache for record companies, threatening to take away their control over the distribution of music. When Diamond Multimedia, the producers of the hugely popular Rio MP3 players, first announced that they would be bringing such a product on to the market, the RIAA (the Recording Industry Association of America, around 250 separate companies) attempted to prevent them from doing so unless certain key requirements were met.

The 1992 Audio Home Recording Act was actually passed the year before, when digital audio tape first arrived. Manufacturers of digital audio equipment were required to pay a royalty to the RIAA, and they also had to introduce a 'flagging system' into their hardware (the Serial Copyright Management System), which would prevent people from running off multiple copies of any given track. But Diamond Multimedia's new MP3 player, it turned out, was not covered by this law, because a 'computer and peripherals exemption' had been written into it. Those who drew the bill up were well aware of the ongoing technological revolution (and the vast future revenues it might involve), and were consequently keen not to 'trap any technology affecting computers in statutory amber'.

So MP3 was given leave to evolve, and the major labels were forced to reassess the situation. For a start, they went hunting, employing specialists to search the web for any pirates who might without permission be giving away or selling music owned by the companies. By October 1999, the RIAA claimed to have busted 80 big sites containing 20,000 illegal MP3 files. Many-high profile pirates have been taken to court, but the net stretches so far and wide that no one can keep up with everything that's going on.

The record companies' problem is simple. They'd like to introduce a proprietary format, which would guarantee they were paid by anyone downloading their music, but it seems that they're just too late. The format used for audio CDs up until now – Redbook – was developed 25 years ago, back when there was no thought of today's advances in home computing power, and thus it has no protecting encryption. This means that every Redbook CD, pretty much every CD produced to date, can be seen as a 'master copy' from which endless MP3 files can be taken.

Of course, the companies would very much like to stop producing Redbook CDs and move on to a different format. Unfortunately, there are now some 550 million CD players out there, all of them using that Redbook format and, if the companies stopped making CDs to suit those players, they'd suffer financially, maybe even be bankrupted. As no way of preventing standard CDs from being converted to MP3 and copied has yet been found, the companies must bow to the inevitable. Every new PC comes with a CD-ROM drive, which means that every new PC owner can copy their own CD collection, upload to the Net and 'share' their music with anyone else. The companies have few friends here. Microsoft themselves have been accused of 'contributing to music piracy' because they enable people to 'mount a CD on a disk drive, pretend [the songs] are computer bits and put them in a file'. Windows 98 does have a built-in MP3 decoder.

Does this spell the end for the music industry as we know it? Maybe not ...

Liquid Audio: the empire strikes back?
Some estimates say that, by 2002, digital music sales will still be as low as $30 million. If that's true, then record companies and anyone else with a vested interest in the status quo (retailers, distributors, etc.) really need have no fears. Retailers, for instance, with their enormous shop-front displays in the very heart of our most populated areas, surely give record companies prime advertising space that simply cannot be ignored. Why would record companies risk such a mutually beneficial relationship for a few thousand sales on the Net?

Well, the reason they might consider adapting their strategies to fully employ the Net (and maybe think about leaving high-street retailing behind for ever) is that the web delivery of music has the potential to be the best thing that ever happened to the industry. Costs might drop, royalties rise, prices fall for consumers, so demand might therefore rise (see Chapter 2). The major labels dare not cede this bright new cyber-territory to independent dealers, unscrupulous pirates and any anti-corporate anarchists with a penchant for 'sharing'.

What they've done is steer clear of the MP3 format and instead explore the commercial digital alternatives. Several companies have been keen to work with them on finding a secure file format for promoting and retailing music over the Net, where users are stopped from 'sharing' songs without paying for them, and the rights of the creators and vendors are thus protected. One can only imagine the reward the industry might offer for a complete solution to the problem. IBM are in the market with their Madison Project, and a2b, a division of the telecommunications giant AT&T, have built a player smart enough to tell whether music has been 'shared' or acquired legitimately.

The frontrunners, though, are the mighty Microsoft with their Windows Media Player, and Liquid Audio. Wherever you roam across the web, you'll find that most major sites dealing in music will facilitate your downloading of a RealPlayer, for audio streaming, an MP3 player (probably WinAmp), and these two players.

Owing to the fabulous success of the MP3 format, Liquid Audio is considered by many to be too little too late. Indeed, it has been rather cruelly called the Betamax to MP3's VHS. But, for such an allegedly 'useless' format, it has made extraordinary inroads.

Liquid Audio was launched in 1996 by venture capitalists, with the intention of offering itself as 'a total service company focusing on the music distribution needs of the record industry'. Quickly, they came up with a format that would allow people to download and store music files only if they had first paid for them. Actually, to be more accurate, you could download and store a Liquid Audio file without paying, but it would self-destruct in a month or so. To keep it for good you'd have to pay.

It was a start, and many record companies went with it. Smashing Pumpkins allowed the public to preview tracks from their latest million-seller via Liquid Audio. The company also made the process extremely convenient for their clients. A record company would simply have to send Liquid a CD, its artwork and whatever extra information was relevant, and Liquid would encode it in a matter of hours. Even the more independently minded labels appreciated this, to the extent that Sub Pop – former home of Nirvana and Mudhoney – did a deal with Liquid to sell their tracks at 88 cents a shot. Liquid are also working with Diamond Multimedia, makers of the hugely popular Rio MP3 players, to create a portable player of their own.

Microsoft have also been busy, and have entered into deals with both the massive search engine Yahoo!, and Musicmaker.com, the leading provider of custom CDs and digitally downloadable music on the Internet. Musicmaker.com are sworn to create the web's single biggest digital download site, while Microsoft have agreed to encode and distribute over 100,000 tracks in their Windows Media format for streaming preview and secure digital downloading. Don't worry for now about which format to obtain. They're all pretty much of a muchness, with no company having produced anything that that has you thinking of a Porsche among Ford Cortinas. For now, there are more tracks available in Liquid Audio and Windows Media Audio, but that may not remain so.

One problem is the uncontrollable nature of the Internet. Though these companies are all searching for a secure alternative to MP3, other techies are currently busting a gut to crack the file formats they come up with. Almost as soon as a2b revealed their 'intelligent' format, then downloadable utilities were offered on the web, allowing you to convert a2b files into MP3.

Digital watermarking is one possibility. Here an audio or video file has a pattern of bits inserted into it, identifying the file's copyright information. Unlike stationers' watermarks, these are intended to remain invisible (or inaudible) so that the bits representing the watermark cannot be spotted and manipulated. Thus the bits are dotted throughout the file, usually disguised as noise. It's hoped that such watermarking will provide some kind of protection against pirating. If you're caught, you're caught as bang-to-rights as if you were covered in blue dye. But you have to be caught first, so with watermarking fear of capture is the only real deterrent.

So the race is on. It's been discovered that consumers, rather than being desperate to get their music for nothing, are actually 'artist-orientated'. They'll do what they need to do to get the tracks they want – be it downloading more software or coughing up the cash. If anything, they prefer not to deal in pirated copies of albums, most of them possessing a basic decency the record companies no doubt appreciate.

In the short term, we'll be watching companies struggling to improve the relatively weedy and time-consuming MP3 format in the hope of total market domination. Others, like Liquid Audio and all the other members of the SDMI (Secure Digital Music Initiative), a movement naturally promoted by the RIAA, will be struggling to find some foolproof means of copyright protection.

In the meantime, the rest of us will continue to enjoy the nonstop technological advances in the transfer of sound direct into our homes. We'll revel in the webcasts that bring gigs to us and take us right into the heart of live interviews. We'll groove to Internet radio stations that let us decide which bands get played and how often. We'll be enthralled as the sites of fans and bands alike bring new revelations, and new meanings to the songs we love. We'll appreciate the massive bargains the Internet is bringing us, and the way it's keeping alive music that might otherwise have been left to degrade in some storeroom.

As far as music goes, the Internet is allowing us to hear more, learn more and share more. It's making everything better. What follows is a guide to how to make it work for you ...

//ADDRESS BOOK

Software and Hardware Sites

One of the greatest sources of information when it comes to talking about the Internet and its future is the business community. If you want to know the new formats and players available (or soon to be available), they'll tell you everything. If you want to know about the deals being done, and, basically, who has the power, always visit the pages about the companies themselves – usually marked 'About Us', or something similar. You'll find extensive press files and relevant links showing you exactly how businesses have interacted and continue to interact to make music on the Internet such a fantastic and ever-evolving thing.

a2b   http://www.a-to-b.com

Part of the mighty AT&T telecommunications empire, fighting hard to find room in what is possibly the cruellest and fastest-moving market on the planet.

Diamond Multimedia   http://www.diamondmm.com

The big boys in the field of portable digital audio players (see RioPort below). Consequently, they have a massive influence on what gives technologically – and thus the gear you get to possess.

Liquid Audio   http://www.liquidaudio.com

In some ways the rival to the MP3 format, Liquid Audio – possibly the Betamax to MP3's VHS – is currently in favour with more paranoid major labels, because of the in-built obsolescence option: e.g. you can have an exclusive Smashing Pumpkins track for a month on your hard drive, then it disappears and you have to buy it if you still want it. Worth downloading the free software here, however, because the quality is great and there are still loads of free tracks out there.

Madison Project   http://www.madisonproject.org

Keep up with IBM's attempt to seize a massive chunk of the digital downloading market.

RealAudio   http://www.realaudio.com

Download the essential software for real audio streaming here. Either get the basic model RealPlayer for free, or pay $29 for a more hi-tech version. They have the Real Jukebox too. Read all the details carefully. You probably won't have to part with any cash to get all the music and videos you desire.

Rio Port   http://www.RioPort.com

The people who bring you the Diamond Rio portable MP3 player shout loudly about it here, but also offer lots of free music in all genres plus, interestingly, a large library of spoken-word material from history to comedy.

Winamp.com   **http://www.winamp.com**
Nullsoft, the company behind the Winamp – the most popular MP3 player – has recently been bought by AOL, and the software is available here to download.

2// THE PRICE IS RIGHT

It's long been common knowledge that, of all products, books and CDs best lend themselves to e-commerce. The music market in particular, already hugely lucrative but for years now in something of a rut, has been expanded by Internet sales and is clearly set to expand further – as was shown by the music giant EMI's being absorbed by Time Warner-AOL, and the burgeoning EMusic.com's purchase of the renowned underground pioneer CDuctive.com. Big business is evidently seeking control of what is rapidly turning into a monstrous money-spinner.

The most obvious reason for this blast-off in e-sales of music is, of course, the price charged. That the record companies and high-street retailers were in sinister cahoots with each other, crushing the independent competition and keeping the price of CDs artificially high, is a much-beloved conspiracy theory. Internet companies have changed all that, breaking down the old pact to the extent that HMV Europe's managing director Brian McLaughlin, in his capacity as chair of the retailers' association board, warned that 'We're obviously responsive to the huge opportunities offered by e-commerce, but we must be alert to record companies possibly paying no regard to the relationship between suppliers and retailers in the UK.' His problem is clear. Net companies almost always undercut high-street prices, and often offer quite eye-popping bargains. Consumers will not ignore them.

For a start, e-retailers have all the advantages enjoyed by traditional mail-order firms, plus a few extra of their own. Where the likes of HMV and Our Price have always endured exorbitant shop rents and overheads, naturally passing these on to the customer, the big e-retailers can send their products out from cheap-to-run, out-of-town warehouses.

Such centralisation of business also cuts out the cost of distribution to branches spread all over the country (or world). Economies of scale dictate that, as the volume of sales grows, so prices fall even further. So successful have many e-retailers been that they can charge for packing and postage (often international) and still be far cheaper than a high-street store.

There are also websites dedicated to finding the best bargains for you. Compare It All Music is listed below. There's also MyTaxi (http://www.mytaxi.co.uk) and ShopGuide (http://www.shopguide.co.uk). Clickmusic (http://www.clickmusic.co.uk) can help out here too but, outside of the United States, bargain-hunters have not proliferated and that's something consumers in the UK have to look forward to. In the meantime, they are still enjoying the notable savings offered by pretty much every music seller on the web.

A bigger change is yet to come. As yet, e-commerce in music has involved the mail-order-like delivery of CDs, tapes and even vinyl. Music suits this type of sale. In contrast to, say, clothing, which may not fit or suit you, with CDs you can be fairly sure what you're getting. But music can also be easily made digital, compressed, uploaded, downloaded and stored. The celebrated MP3 format and new alternatives like Liquid Audio allow us to build collections of CD-quality music on our own hard drives, to be played through the computer system. There is also already a wide range of small, portable and unarguably cool-looking MP3 players available (intended to replace the Walkman), to which you may transfer your favourite music. As technology improves and more and more consumers possess the requisite hardware, it's likely that most music will be delivered digitally – the merging of EMI, Time-Warner and AOL unarguably points to that.

High-street retailers are attempting to adapt. Such is the quality of service now provided by many e-retailers that they must adapt or die. The most successful high-street shops turn themselves into music superstores, offering CDs, tapes, vinyl, books, posters, T-shirts, videos, computer games, live performances, celebrity autograph-signing sessions, the lot. Yet, as many e-retailers offer all of this at a reduced price, they'll have to go further. Just as cybercafés are springing up all over, providing coffee, snacks and a terminal, so music shops will surely come to offer something similar but typically funkier. They'll market themselves as meeting places and cool hangouts where you can listen to anything and purchase from a gargantuan, computer-based back catalogue, either buying full albums or compiling your own from a choice of absolutely everything. It's actually been mooted that e-commerce – aligned with such a focus on comfort and atmosphere, where clubs, bars, coffee houses, galleries and shops are all combined and angled towards particular sections of society – may bring about an amazing and unexpected resurgence in local shopping.

Buying music on the Internet: what to expect

There can be no doubt that, for genuine lovers of music, the Internet is a boon of fantastic proportions. Where before you may have asked your local record store attendant for a new release only to be blankly and ignorantly informed that 'Sorry, it's deleted', now an awesome range of music stretching back nearly a hundred years has suddenly become easily available. And the scope can only increase as old recordings are gradually digitally remastered and made available – easier now, as retailers need have only one copy on file, rather than take the risk of having 10,000 CDs gathering dust in some storeroom. Thanks to ever-improving search engines and a link-up between specialist stores made possible only by the Internet, if there's only one remaining copy of the record you desire and it's sitting in a bargain bin in a sleaze-pit store in the backstreets of Soweto, you can find it and buy it.

Music from the twenties and thirties, contemporary pop and rock, rap and R&B, jazz, classical, psychedelia, film scores and show tunes, all are open to you like never before. You just have to click on the right button. Naturally, if you're on the lookout for Sowetan rarities, you're probably going to have to pay through the nose. Most of us, though, are will be catered for quickly, securely and inexpensively by one of the larger e-retailers.

And everyone is getting in on the act – major record companies, traditional supermarkets like Woolworth, and magazines like *NME*. There are huge e-stores, such as Amazon and Virgin, dealing in pretty much everything. There are the likes of CD Universe and Audiostreet, dealing in bargain sales. Beanos, Abbey Records and many others offer second-hand goods and rarities. And there are a host of specialist labels and shops delving deeper than ever before into the archives of every genre. You can compile your own CD at Musicmaker.com (http://www.musicmaker.com), or sample the wares of hundreds of thousands of unsigned bands on the many MP3 sites now up and running. The choice is absurd.

Such has been the time, money and effort put in to many of these ventures that shopping really couldn't be any easier, even for those wholly unfamiliar with the ways of the web. Casual visitors to, for example, the American giant CD Now (http://www.cdnow.com), with its range of far in excess of 500,000 items, can see immediately and clearly from the homepage what's on offer and what procedures need to be followed (you can follow them in seven different languages too). You can catch up on the latest news, reviews (from the excellent *Rolling Stone* magazine), and interviews with the elevated likes of Nanci Griffith. Big bargains are splashed, such as Christina Aguilera's debut album at only £8. Gift certificates may be purchased – to be emailed to the recipient within one day of payment, or on any day you select.

Those hot to shop can go immediately to the Customise Your Own CD section, or begin to browse the well-labelled, genre-based archives, hearing clips from albums in either RealAudio or MPEG. Those wishing to download music are offered a free liquid player, for both Windows and Macintosh, and there are hundreds of tracks available from big-name artists – those advertised at the time of writing included Smashing Pumpkins, Elliott Smith and Sixpence None The Wiser.

And it's safe, too

New customers are welcomed politely and guided expertly. Having clicked on 'Create Account', you are shown the ropes in the simplest of terms. Orders are placed using Netscape's SSL (Secure Socket Layer) encryption, which is the Internet standard for secure transactions and is built into all major browsers and web servers. Basically, this delivers the details of your transaction with the retailer in a code that cannot be broken by an outside party, so no one can hack in there and steal your credit-card details. SSL comes in two strengths, 40-bit and 128-bit, the numbers referring to the length of the 'session key' generated by every encrypted trans-action. The longer the key, the harder it is to break the encryption code. Most browsers support 40-bit, but the latest (including

Netscape Communicator 4.0) allow users to use 128-bit, which is trillions of times stronger.

Forty-bit is safe enough though, leading the *Philadelphia Enquirer* to report: 'In 1997, there were no reports of credit-card information being stolen on the World Wide Web during a transfer of information over a Secure Socket Layer line, the kind of line used by Netscape Navigator and Microsoft Explorer. There were no slip-ups. None.'

Look to the bottom corner of your browser and make sure there is a tiny locked padlock. This tells you that you're on a Secure Server and can feel free to type in your credit-card details, safe in the knowledge that you stand more chance of having your card details stolen when buying goods over the phone, or even in a shop or eatery. In the case of CD Now, and many other retailers, if you do not wish to fill in your card details thus, you can telephone, fax or email them direct to the retailer.

Your order information and purchase history may furthermore be protected by a password. If you forget this, CD Now will first verify your ID, then email the password to the address you have listed in your CD Now account.

Now you're shopping, with your own virtual shopping cart – usually a box that tells you which items you've chosen, the quantity, the format (tape, CD, etc.), how much they cost and how much they would cost if they weren't so unbelievably cheap here. Time to wander through the vast, simply ordered catalogues. Each album will probably be presented with artwork and a track listing, some or all of the tracks being highlighted so you can click and play to see if it grabs you. There may also be biographies of the artists concerned, discographies, reviews, photos, and some retailers have bonus features. CD Universe, for instance, allow you to chat with fellow customers and even co-browse with them, so you can shop with your friends if you wish.

Be careful at this stage. Almost everything will seem cheap, you can be taken aback by the sheer numbers of CDs you love and must possess right now, and the tendency is to immediately and grievously overspend. Play the field. It may seem cheap, but it may be even cheaper elsewhere. This is presently one of the great joys of e-retailing – the competition is frightening. Watch out especially for postage and packing charges. Some firms deliver packages free if you spend over a certain amount: the bigger ones are always reasonable. But smaller concerns do sometimes overcharge for this service, which quickly turns a bargain into a rip-off.

Read the details. CD Now promise to let you return any item within 30 days of delivery for a refund (minus shipping and handling). A refund or replacement will be supplied upon the return of any damaged items (no extra shipping charges). If you're told as you order that an item is in stock when it actually isn't, they will ship it to you later at no extra cost, and you are charged for your goods on shipment. Again, read the details – they can vary wildly. CD Now are exceptionally efficient and trustworthy – others may not be.

Now that's what you call music
One further liberation of the music buyer brought about by the Internet is, as we saw earlier, the chance to compile your own CDs. How many albums do you possess where half the tracks are mere fillers? And how many bands only ever write one popular track before disappearing without trace? The Primitives, anyone? Or Daisy Chainsaw? Need we mention the unforgettable Joe Dolce? No, compilations are the bee's knees for the casual music listener,

and are a boon for the serious aficionado too. And there are many sites springing up that allow you to compile CDs from almighty lists of classic tunes by famous outfits, in much the same way as MP3 sites provide an outlet for unsigned bands.

The most thrusting of these sites is the aforementioned Musicmaker.com, and it gives you the best idea of what these sites have to offer, and how they're generally set out and navigated. This site is mammoth, and incredibly easy to move around. The homepage points you to charts of the Top 100 most popular artists and tracks (so, if you wish, you can be just like everyone else). Then there are albums newly compiled by Musicmaker themselves, and suggested compilations you might like. Once you've set up your account and started purchasing, thereby giving them some idea of your tastes, they'll also suggest songs and artists you might like.

Finding your favourite acts is a simple question of scrolling down the lists of genres, then scrolling again for the specific performers. The list of genres is almost comically comprehensive, including Christian, Boogie Woogie, French Oldies, Hanukkah, Patriotic and even Zydeco. If you do not have the appropriate software for listening and downloading, Musicmaker link you to sites providing you with everything you need – a RealPlayer G2 (for RealAudio), a Liquid Music Player (for Liquid Audio), a WinAmp (for MP3) and Microsoft's Windows Media Player. So simple it almost hurts.

Musicmaker's lists are enormous, their aim being to make available over a million tracks. Marketing deals with both AOL and Tunes.com will no doubt keep their profile high. Naxos have made 1,200 classical albums available to them, while deals with the likes of the EMI, TVT and Zomba labels, give them access to the works of hipsters such as Nine Inch Nails, Speech, Sevendust and Guided By Voices and multi-million-sellers like Britney Spears, R. Kelly and the Backstreet Boys. You can bet that, in cross-promotional exercises, these artists will soon be offering tracks exclusively on Musicmaker, and that competition with Musicmaker for overall control of digital downloading will be fierce. In the future, you'll be well advised to keep your eyes peeled for the latest corporate mergers or marketing deals – they'll make a big difference to how and where your favourite band's music is made available.

Shopping with Musicmaker.com is very easy. You can click to view and edit your CD, to personalise it with 'unique' labels and imprints on the jewel box, and to delete tracks or to finish it off. Add, Play and Info buttons are self-explanatory. At the time of writing the first five songs will cost you $4.95 ($9.95 if you're outside the United States), with each additional track costing $1. There's a limit of 20 tracks, or 70 minutes of music. Don't worry about going over the limit: they let you know where you stand as you go along.

Musicmaker are keen to let you know that theirs was the first totally automated system for the sale of music over the Internet. Once you've given your credit-card details (this is very much a secure system) and finalised the content and ordering of your CD, you click once and the manufacturing process begins. Your CD will be made up, on the day you order it (Musicmaker's software has over 100,000 lines of custom code), at a 'specialized central production facility' in Virginia, and mailed to you. Here state-of-the-art CD-R writers knock out customer disks at around ten per hour per recorder, which is about eight times the usual playing rate. Musicmaker are very keen to let you know that the tracks on your CD are exactly the same as the original – there is none of the sound quality degradation that always occurs when copying one CD from another.

Unbelievably hi-tech? Maybe this is just the start of it. As more and more of us become connected to the Net and use it to purchase CDs and digital downloads, so competition for that expanding market will force companies to provide ever-improving services. Check out the final chapter of this book for some of the possibilities currently being planned or tested (some of them, of course, involving Musicmaker.com). But rest assured that, when it comes to pursuing our cash, big companies, like sharks, never rest. We ain't seen nothing yet.

//ADDRESS BOOK

General Stores

Amazon   **http://www.amazon.co.uk**
The mother of them all – Amazon's UK site offers a huge range of greatly discounted pop CDs, many with Real Audio sound clips and full track listings. Simple ordering and reasonable delivery prices help too.

Artist Direct Network –   **http://www.ubl.com**
The Ultimate Band List
A reliable shop site with detailed information courtesy of those nice All Music Guide people. The site is so much more than just an online store that it warrants a mention as a good starter site too: up-to-date news, features, links and audio clips. Oh, and the CD prices are quite reasonable too.

Audiostreet   **http://www.audiostreet.co.uk**
Described by some as the premiere online music store – hard to see why. A few Real Audio samples, but no track listings, no artwork

reproductions, and the news features are sometimes a week old. The prices are high-street, the delivery free and all credit-card transactions are secure.

Blackstar   http://www.blackstar.co.uk

Mainly videos, and not much music either. Slow, too.

Bol.Com   http://www.bol.com

The music part of this store, which started life as a bookshop, has good editorial content and full track listings with audio sound clips. However, the stock has glaring omissions, and the prices are often more than you would pay on the high street.

Borders   http://www.borders.com

A packed online version of the US shop. The music section allows an expert search for those who have only a vague recollection of the name of the CDs they are looking for. Very useful. Cheap in the way US shops tend to be, but with the added downside of transatlantic shipping costs.

Borrow Or Rob   http://www.borroworrob.com

Very fast and efficient service from this US/UK shop. There is a useful bargain-hunter facility allowing you to click on either I'm Skint or I'm Loaded. Search for anything by artist, though, not title. Free delivery for orders over £5.

Boxman   http://www.boxman.co.uk

Fairly good service from this UK site, with a large catalogue of current releases and a search resource that works better for artists and song titles than it does for album titles.

CD Now   http://www.cdnow.com

A US-based shop with great biographies courtesy of the All Music Guide, and fast connections to any CD you want. UK releases are very expensive, sometimes as much as $27, but there are useful genre-specific Buyers' Guides and MP3 samples before you buy. Shipping is $5 anywhere in the world.

CD Paradise
http://www.cdparadise.com

Part of WH Smith, it prides itself on its security. The prices are pretty competitive and the selection of current and back catalogue is extensive. Goodbye, high street?

CD Rack
http://www.cdrack.co.uk

Two hundred thousand titles and a lot of news links, trivia and games. The shop is secure but really offers very little in the way of reviews or track listings.

CD World
http://www.cdworld.com

Allegedly the largest CD online store. Ask for anything, even reasonably priced imports and unreasonably priced Japanese imports.

Cheap Or What! CDs
http://www.cow.co.uk

Actually not always as cheap as the big discount stores, but postage is free in the UK.

Compare It All Music
http://www.compareitall.com

A reliable, if slightly US-centric, guide to finding the best deals on the web for CDs, searching through over 30 retailers.

Entertainment Express
http://www.entexpress.com

Owned by the people who own Woolworth, this store offers a safe and free delivery of your shopping. The emphasis is on retail rather than editorial, and the prices are more high-street than e-street – in other words, not cheaper. Fast delivery is guaranteed.

Getmusic.Com
http://www.getmusic.com

A joint venture between two major record labels, BMG and Universal, Getmusic is enthusiastically focused on new releases from these labels. Fine if you want Sheryl Crow, Beck, or the Foo Fighters but the search facility has not heard of Travis and wants $23 for the current Chemical Brothers album. Shipping is $2.99 for item one followed by 79 cents per subsequent item. In the US.

Go Music   http://www.gomusic.freeserve.co.uk
UK-based retailer with a fair selection including vinyl, as well as the usual CDs and minidiscs. Not many track listings or much biographical information, though.

HMV   http://www.hmv.co.uk
A replica of the high-street shop (just music and games, no books) complete with all the two-CDs-for-one-style special offers. Fortunately, there is no queue of tourists in front of you at the checkout.

Jungle   http://www.jungle.com
One of the very best UK stores. The magic number here appears to be £9.87, which would procure the Travis, Shania Twain or Westlife album as well as many other current chart toppers. Aside from many great one-off deals, the catalogue is well laid out and extensive, there is free delivery, it's 100 per cent secure and a big snake greets you on every page.

K-TEL   http://www.ktel.com
Not just the usual good-value compilations that this US company have been producing since the 60s, but a store rivalling the big guys. There is no news or detailed biographies of the artists but every item is discounted and there is an auction facility and other fun K-Tel stuff. Check out the kitsch, old TV ads in Real Video.

MGVC   http://www.imvs.com
There are 230,000 of the latest titles, and a good back-catalogue selection. Sometimes hard to navigate and certainly not a store

that offers you anything more than shopping for hits or CDs you already know about.

Net Megastore   **http://www.net-megastore.co.uk**
A pretty basic UK-based shop site which offers free delivery to those in the UK and Channel Islands. It's quite slow with surprising stock omissions.

101CD   **http://www.101cd.com**
Fast and efficient service from this UK-based site. A stock of over a million CDs, games and videos plus another 500,000 imports. Pure shopping, though: no biogs or info or links.

Pentagon CD   **http://www.pentagon.net**
Claiming to have the cheapest selection of CDs on the web, they are fairly competitively priced, and all CDs are categorised by genre, making it easy to search.

Powerplay Direct   **http://www.powerplaydirect.co.uk**
Fast and efficient online store which is secure and pretty good value too. Not much there apart from the stock – no news/reviews, etc. You can phone them if they don't have something in stock.

Quickmusic.com   **http://www.quickmusic.com**
Providing a catalogue of over 150,000 titles, with quick searching and competitive prices, this US site offers track listings for every album and Real Audio streamed samples. Album reviews courtesy of the All Music Guide as well.

Record Store   **http://www.recordstore.co.uk**
Everything you could possibly want from a hip dance store with none of the snobby elitism that usually goes with the territory. Almost Heineken-like, so unexpected is the refreshment.

Sam The Record Man   **http://www.samscd.com**

This promising new site offers a specialist search for the CD of your choice. The prices are reasonable too.

Shopsafe   **http://www.shopsafe.co.uk**

Designed to be an alternative to a search engine, so gives lists of every type of online store, all of which are secure for online transactions.

WH Smith   **http://www.whsmith.co.uk**

A few clicks to get to the music section, but once you're there it's a good site with news headlines from several other reputable sites like Click, TOTP and Drum And Bass Arena. Easier to use as a search engine than to find out if WH Smith stock what you're after – often they don't.

Tower   **http://www.tower.com**

Fantastic. One of the most popular sites for music shopping. The prices are as cheap as if you were in the actual US shop. Search by artist, song title, even record label. Make your own CD as well. Each album has a full track listing and Real Audio streamed samples. Shipping within the US is $4.95 for delivery in two days; outside it's best to buy in bulk at $20 for up to three CDs.

Tower Europe   **http://www.towereurope.com**

Not quite as sexy as the US site, but it boasts very acceptable prices, full track listings and sound clips.

Tunes.com   **http://www.tunes.com**

A shop cunningly disguised as a webzine, Tunes is friendly, useful and informative, with Real Audio clips for every album selection, video feeds, and a biography section. Full track listings for all records too.

Virgin Megastore   http://www.virginmega.com

The US wing for the international retail outfit with a great range of everything you want on disc or tape. Not much content, however, and shipping outside the US costs a whopping $7.29 for item one, followed by $1.99 for each subsequent item. In the US, delivery takes up to eight days, outside up to two weeks.

Yalplay   http://www.yalplay.com

A slightly confusing store, which takes a while to feel at home with. There are the usual Top Ten choices and discounted stuff, but no track listings and little information. You will find a lot of sites linked to this one (the silly name comes from the word 'play' backwards).

Make your own CDs

CDuctive   http://www.cductive.com

Like Musicmaker, this has a weak selection of major artists, but CDuctive focuses on more new music with interesting hip-hop, alternative rock and electronic sections. Prices are $4.99 for the first track and 99 cents for every other after that.

Musicmaker.com   http://www.musicmaker.com

A Digital Download Internet Shop, ambitious and straightforward. Buy tracks from their ever-expanding library, which, thanks to deals with EMI, Zomba and TVT, has 60s and 70s hits and a growing number of contemporary artists. It'll cost you $12.95 for five tracks outside the US and Canada; each extra track costs $1, and don't forget shipping costs. Hmm, perhaps a little pricey for those outside the US.

Specialist Shops

Action Records   http://www.action-records.co.uk
Split into dance and rock sections, this stocks a good range of indie
material on CD, vinyl and cassette.

Blockbuster.com   http://www.blockbuster.com
The US arm of this massive swelling organisation – great for
soundtracks but does not currently sell non-movie-related music.

CD Baby   http://www.cdbaby.com
Boasting a list of hard-to-find albums by lots of terribly obscure
artists – possibly hard to find because no one wants them.
Potentially great, but limited in stock.

CD Xpress   http://www.cdxpress.co.uk
A store focusing on 70s rock reissues and all that is Twin-Guitar
Mayhem.

Cob Records   http://www.elfyn.ndirect.co.net
Welsh-based leading independent record dealer, specialising in
used and new CDs, they will buy or part-exchange your unwanted
stuff, too. Also on the site is an exhaustive trawl through every UK
independent record shop that's online. Very useful.

Coda Music   http://www.codamusic.co.uk
These sell instruments but mostly CDs – folk, Scottish, blues, world
music, country, 'anything Celtic'. If they haven't got it, they'll find it.

Dance DJ Direct   http://www.dance-dj-direct.com
Concentrating on UK dance, this is both shop and news service.

Everything English   http://www.everythingenglish.com
Exactly what it says – reminiscent of one of those touristy stores
around Carnaby Street. This US store sells new and used CDs as well

as T-shirts, stickers and posters of all your favourite English bands from the Beatles to, er, Discharge.

Forced Exposure   http://www.forcedexposure.com
A US specialist online store with detailed reviews of all new releases. Records stocked are mainly obscure American and European alternative bands with a bias towards quality reissues of hard-to-find collectables. The staff write about their own personal choices, too, which is refreshing.

German Music Express   http://www.musicexpress.com
Fantastically well-organised CD store specialising in hard-to-find music – not just CD albums, but back-catalogue singles too, and all at reasonable prices. No track listings, unfortunately.

Global Audiophile   http://www.globalaudiophile.com
A well-put-together specialist store for the selective collector of old and rare classical, jazz, big-band, film and soundtracks, opera and nostalgia.

Hard To Find   http://www.hardtofind.co.uk
Dance-orientated vinyl and CD shop, packed with stuff that is, well, what the name suggests.

Hemisphere   http://www.hemisphere.nl
A very good independent-record retailer with an amazingly fast search system that will find even the most obscure old rubbish from the early 80s. Prices are OK too.

In Sound   http://www.insound.com
Another US alternative-music store, this one has a library of exclusive photos, as well as a regularly updated 'Insoundoff' column, which is always entertaining and informative. Search for a style – from garage rock revival to shoegazing to jungle – and try not to max all your credit cards.

Musicspot http://www.musicspot.com

Excellent for rock music. Provides reviews and CD info, and allows you compile your own albums.

Nervous Records http://www.nervous.co.uk

Freaky SFX, strange hairdos, and more psychobilly than a fellow can stand.

Other Music http://www.othermusic.com

The coolest of New York's independent record stores goes online with a genre-led search engine to find all your hard-to-find, specialist desirables, from Krautrock to psychedelia. Shipping is $4.50 per 1-4 items in the US and $8 in the rest of the world.

Parasol Records http://www.parasol.com

Another good US indie record store, this time one that has grown from the label of the same name famed for releasing 'Your Woman' by White Town. But don't be fooled: the specialist flavour here is predominantly US college rock and alternative country music.

Past Perfect http://www.pastperfect.com

Concentrating on remastered tunes from the twenties to the forties – Noël Coward, George Gershwin, Cole Porter. Ah yes, those were the days, when men were men, women were women and music was music ...

Razorcuts Custom CD http://www.razorcuts.com/default1.asp

Compile your own CD from a vast range, including opera, lounge, jazz, classical, film and show tunes.

Rough Trade Shop http://www.roughtrade.com

New alternative releases, staff choices, used records, vinyl, gig and event listings and concert tickets, as well the nice friendly atmosphere you get in the Talbot Road shop itself. The search engine is easy to use and the new-release section is displayed in thumbnail pictures, which makes it easier to spot the record you're looking for. They will email you with the week's new releases, if you want.

Vinyl Exchange   http://www.vinylexchange.co.uk
Indie, dance and funk on vinyl. Check the catalogue, then email to confirm the availability of the single or album you desire.

Voiceprint Group   http://www.voiceprint.co.uk
Purveyors of old-school prog, folk and psychedelia. Gong, Fairport Convention, Wishbone Ash – Lord, where does the time go?

Wax City   http://www.waxcity.com
A US store site that's laid out to give you the week's new dance releases by genre (house/hip-hop/drum and bass, etc.) and the opportunity to hear clips in Real Audio.

Y2K Music   http://www.y2k-music.co.uk
Highlighting new acts from rock to classical. Listen to samples on RealAudio's Jukebox, then buy if you feel the need.

Second-hand and Collectables

Abbey Records   http://www.abbeyrecords.com
A reliable and well-respected used-CD and vinyl site – bargain prices, a varied selection and above all, easy to use.

Beanos   http://www.beanos.co.uk
Established in 1975, this fantastic store in Croydon is crammed with over 2 million used CDs and records. The website is little more than a guide to the goodies in the shop so there's no online ordering service. You can, however, email them and become one of the hundreds of enquiries they deal with daily via their mail-order service.

Cellophane Square   http://www.cellophane.com
These both buy and sell CDs, and the catalogue can be down-loaded and read offline. Excellent for US material.

Discophile   http://www.discophile.com
Search the 9,000-strong database for used-CD obscurities or cheaper versions of what is already out there. Some surprising discoveries – worth checking if you're hunting for something in particular.

Forever Vinyl   http://www.forvevervinyl.com
A friendly and helpful home-made site from one Scott Neuman of New Jersey and his dog Max – the official record cleaner who begs, 'Let me lick your record!' They have been buying and selling vinyl for 20 years and have over 2,000,000 items in stock. You can call as well as email, although not after 10.30 p.m. local time, when Max is sleeping.

Intoxica   http://www.demon.co.uk/intoxica
Rough Trade's favourite second-hand record shop – a London-based vinyl specialist which deals in used groove, alternative and jazz records. The prices are reasonable and the stock extensive. Get hunting!

Music And Video Exchange   http://www.mveshops.co.uk
The Notting Hill-based London Mecca of second-hand-everything-goes online. A fabulous selection of vinyl rarities as well as posters and cultural ephemera, it is particularly good for film soundtracks. The prices are fair-ish and they will search for any item you are looking for.

Off The Record   http://www.otrvinyl.com
Well presented and easy-to-use site for rare and collectable records – if you're desperate you will go anywhere, but this is a good place to start.

Second Spin   http://www.secondspin.com
Claims to be 'the world's largest buyer and seller of used CDs, movies and DVDs'. US-based, but ships everywhere, and prices can plummet to under $3.

Sweet Memories   http://www.vinylrecords.co.uk
Fifteen thousand vinyl rarities stretching back to the fifties.

Visual Vinyl   http://www.visualvinyl.co.uk
Rarities and promos, used vinyl and CDs – this one's a must for rockers and metal-heads everywhere.

World Party Music   http://www.wpmusic.com
A catalogue of 150,000 new and used CDs. You can buy as well as sell via this store. Little biographical information, but a great selection of hard-to-find titles from both indie and major labels.

3//LOOKING FOR MR GOODTUNE

Though it may disagree with the elitist in you, you must accept that, as far as music goes, you are probably not entirely original in your interests. Whatever acts you like, you will doubtless be able to read about them on at least one of the billion-plus web pages currently running.

This is, of course, A Good Thing. One of the great boons of the Internet is the way it makes massive amounts of information available to us all. Before, if you wanted to know absolutely everything about a band, you could only hope that a book had been written about them, or that some journalist might decide to interview them. You could perhaps find out the rude basics from the few rock encyclopedias available, or maybe take the trouble to visit the offices of some music magazine and delve through their (usually poorly organised) archives. Basically, if your idol wasn't already famous, you had a problem.

In fact, everything was a problem if you didn't live in one of the Western world's largest conurbations. Musicians couldn't find affordable equipment or people to play with (uhuh huh huh). Shops never stocked the music you wanted, and ordering it was ludicrously expensive. Everything was a pain.

The Internet has changed all this. Now there's so much information available you couldn't possibly wade through it all and, if you tried ... well, that way madness lies.

What you need is a guide, someone to lead you through the seemingly endless morass of rumour, gossip, potted histories, sound files, picture galleries, gig listings, features and reviews old and new and all manner of eulogies and senseless attacks that most artists unwittingly provoke. Never fear, there's plenty of help out there, and much of it is far more impressive than the sites you're trying to reach.

The title for each of these guides changes depending on who you ask. A year ago, the definitions were clearer. There were search engines, which tried to link you to every bit of information anywhere on the web. Then there were search directories, which were more particular, limiting themselves to a few hundred thousand links – each of these having been checked out by one of their employees. And then there were portals, which provided their own content, and linked to everything, with the intention being to make their site your starting point whatever you wanted to know or buy. These days, so ambitious and technologically advanced are most search-engine sites that they almost all merit the 'portal' moniker.

How to search – a basic guide

All search engine sites are similar in one vital respect: they all have an immediately recognisable search entry field, a simple block inside which you type the subject of your search. Beside the field will be a button marked 'Search' or 'Go' or something appropriate, upon which you click when you're ready. Hitting 'Return' will usually do the same job.

The way most search engines work is this: using automatic software, they create an index of sites. These automatic programs – called spiders, or robots, or crawlers, owing to their relentless creeping about the web – are constantly digging up new websites, recording their addresses, and delving through their pages to discover exactly what they're about. When you type a name or subject into the search entry field, your query is sent off to the distant computer, where the search-engine software resides. This zooms through the millions of websites in its index and pulls out anything that matches your request. Everything is then ordered, usually with the most relevant items first, and set out on your screen, all in a matter of seconds.

You'll be told how many matches have come up, and the number can reach into the millions. Then you simply begin scrolling downwards, reading the little blurbs accompanying the link to each site to see if they're quite what you're after. Sometimes the spider will have pulled out this info; often the page designer will have included specific info to help the spider to index accurately. Read carefully. Sometimes a site will be cited as relevant purely because of the number of times your search entry is mentioned, and this can send you to any number of rabid fan sites.

Once you've scrolled to the bottom of the page, you'll find a button marked 'More' or sometimes 'Next'. This will take you to the next set of links. It's standard to get ten links to each page, though some search engines allow you to increase that number. You can keep clicking 'More', slipping deeper and deeper into irrelevance, till all matches are exhausted. It's said that only about 20 per cent of websites are indexed by search engines. Nevertheless, as said, you can still end up wasting plenty of time.

One trick is to narrow the search. Some search engines, like AskJeeves (**http://www.askjeeves.com**) are so bright they let you type in a straight question, like 'Can I see every show of Metallica's European tour?', and will turn up reasonable answers (plus a few crazy ones – try it for a laugh). Most others work better if you tell them exactly what you want to know.

There are some helpful techniques you can learn easily. You can refine your searches on many search engines simply by using the symbols + and -. Say you're trying to remember the name of the song Metallica recorded with Marianne Faithfull. Putting quote marks around each name narrows the search. If you key in "Marianne Faithfull", the engine will stick to the point and not seek out every mention of the words Marianne and Faithfull on the web. (Note that I've used double quotes here and not the 'single' quotation marks that are this book's preferred style. You'll find this is what search engines use.) Now put a + between "Metallica" and "Marianne Faithfull", so the engine will dig up only those sites that mention the two names together. Always use quotes when searching for specific names, and for famous sayings like "Who breaks a butterfly upon a wheel?"

You can also narrow your search using the nifty and catchily named Boolean operators. These are the words AND, OR and NOT which you place between your search entries (in capital letters, as here) to obvious effect. Perhaps you're pretty sure the song has the word 'Memory' in the title. Key in "Metallica" AND "Marianne Faithfull" AND "memory". The double quotes demand that the engine provides only links to sites where all three queries are mentioned. And there you have it – The Memory Still Remains. Grrr.

A nice threesome

If you're on a mission, with no time to browse, then Google (http://www.google.com) is a good bet. It was founded in 1998 by two Stanford Ph.D students, and its name is a play on the term 'googol', which, as you doubtless know already, refers to the number represented by a 1 followed by 100 zeroes and was coined by Milton Sirotta, nephew of the US mathematician Edward Kasner. The name's supposed to refer to the company's intention of organising all the information (zeroes and ones) in the world, and Google does already deal with over 3.5 million searches a day – its popularity and growing reputation being due to its sleek yet colourful design, its impossible speed and gratifying effectiveness. No, really. This is one even the professionals are talking about.

Where most portals and search engines greet you with a splurge of links and information (they have no choice, they do so much), Google's homepage is dominated by two search entry fields marked 'Google Search' and 'I'm Feeling Lucky'. The first gives a general search, the second immediately takes you to the number-one site turned up by the search.

The search engine itself is based on PageRank technology, which orders matching sites by 'objectively measuring' their importance. To do this, Google interprets a link from, say, Page A to Page B as a vote by Page A for Page B, and counts up all the votes for each page (a vote from an important page weighing more than another). Thus it works out a site's relevance to your query by solving an equation of 500 million variables and over 2 billion terms. Mind-boggling.

The results are excellently laid out too, with an excerpt from each web page and your search terms highlighted in boldface – so you can tell if Google's got the gist and if you need to alter the terms of the search. Our search for Kate Bush resulted in 20,700 matches in 0.04 of a second. Quite rightly, Gaffaweb (http://www.gaffa.org) was at the top, followed by Cloudbusting (http://www. cogsci.ed.ac.uk/~rjc/hyper_cloud/kate_bush.html) and all the biggest and most renowned Bush sites. One excellent links page (http://www.charm.net/~totoro/katelink.html) even allowed you to download the music La Bush did for the Fruitopia commercials.

On top of their straight search, Google also provide two added extras beneath each link. One is a cached link. It's possible that the current content of the page you're being linked to is of no use to you, since pages are changing all the time. Click on the cached link to see the page content when Google first indexed the site. That might be helpful. Then there's a GoogleScout button, which, if the link provided is along the right lines but not quite enough, will link you to around a dozen sites with similar content. And, sorry to repeat it, but it's all so fast.

If you're not looking for anything in particular, one of the huge portals now running will be a big eye-opener for you. Yahoo! (http:uk.news.yahoo.com/m/music.html), once a simple directory, has expanded outwards at a terrifying rate. The homepage includes the lot – world news, stores, recreation and sports info, arts and humanities etc. – but Yahoo! was always well respected for its coverage of film and music. Click on the link marked 'Music' and see how much there is to browse through: sections on reference, trivia, events, polls, discographies, theory, software, hardware. Fantastic stuff, and very easy to navigate. The only shame is the cluttering effect of all the advertising.

Maybe a better bet, and certainly one for the future, is the fast-moving Clickmusic site (http://www.clickmusic.co.uk). This is a 'vortal', or a vertical portal, i.e. a portal that specialises in one subject, in this case music. Just looking at it makes your head swim. There are links marked audio, celebrities, lyrics, magazines, music videos, record labels, clubs, directories, DJs, webcasts, sound files, instruments, chat/forums, competitions, games, interviews, radio, comedy (and humour), not to mention the best online bargains and MP3s. You can search for artists by name – the results being very clear and detailed, with each link carrying a helpful review – or look through alphabetised lists to see what takes your fancy. They'll also take you to the Best Of rock, reggae, indie, dance and techno sites, which is ideal for the casual visitor.

Since no search engine has indexed absolutely everything on the web, their results will inevitably vary. For this reason, many people prefer to employ metasearchers. These basically search the searchers by passing on your query to all the major search engines and directories and then gathering together all the results. This is clearly a deeper search, but not necessarily better suited to your needs.

Music databases: all we're ever looking for
As shown by the Encyclopaedia Britannica's taking to the web, big databases work brilliantly here. No need for tree-felling, expensive printing or ludicrously difficult distribution. Just update as you please – no more wrecked backs for anyone.

Within music, people have been very quick in their efforts to become the pre-eminent database, and they've come into it from all different angles. The famous Amazon.com (http://www. amazon.com/music), for instance, has grown from being a retailer to a major source of information, spending years and millions of dollars gathering in-depth features and attempting to review every album ever made. *Rolling Stone* (http://www.rollingstone.com) came in the other way, using its back issues to build its stock of online information, then adding reams of extras, and turning itself into a shop and a host for webcasts. Unlike most websites, *Rolling Stone* also has fact-checkers. Elsewhere, the Ultimate Band List (http://ubl.com) widened to become a near-portal, while SonicNet (http://www.sonicnet.com) is, among many other things, a major link to Internet radio stations and can also dig up info on pretty much any band you mention.

All these sites have different styles and angles of approach. For instance, for deadly serious explanations of absolutely everything, try About.com (http://home.about.com). Oh, and if they start using web terms you don't understand, go to Webopedia (http://www.webopedia.com). It's really helpful.

Mailing lists and newsgroups

Finally, you might check music mailing lists and newsgroups. Mailing lists are like serious discussion groups. There are now around 100,000 of them, each with its own subject, and many involve music. Basically, you add your email address to any list you choose and, when you feel you have something to add to the discussion, you mail your message to the site's controllers and they pass it on to everyone else on the list. They can be a little dry but may suit anoraks, students and band members. You can discover these via most search engines, or maybe allow yourself to be guided by a bona fide list site like the well-named Liszt (http://www.liszt.com). Instructions on how to join each list will be readily available.

Newsgroups are a tad different. Indeed, these are known as the bad boys of the web, being (very) basic forums for discussion where anyone can rant, howl and voice even the most disagreeable of opinions on pretty much any subject. There are over 30,000 of them, collectively known as the Usenet. How to obtain and configure a news reader so you can join in is well covered in this book's sister volume **The Virgin Guide to the Internet**; but, as Microsoft and Netscape include one in their free web-browser programs, chances are you're already tooled up. Either look for the 'Read News' link on Microsoft's Outlook Express, or select 'Messenger' from the Communicator menu in Netscape Navigator.

There are also alternative helpers to guide you around newsgroups. If you have a PC, try Agent at http://www.forteinc.com/getfa/getfa.htm, or if you're a Maccie, go to Newswatcher at http://www.best.com/~smfr/mtnw. On top of this, there are websites you can visit for deep conversations that are newsgroup-like in their seriousness. Try RemarQ at http://www.remarq.com and Talkway at http://www.talkway.com.

Newsgroups are pretty similar to email programs in the way they appear and operate. On one side you'll see a list of newsgroups, on the other a list of title lines from all the latest postings. Click on the title line to read the whole message. When a message has provoked a discussion or argument, it's said to have begun a 'new thread' and has a little square beside it. Click on the square to see all the different opinions it's drawn from folk around the world. Sending a message to the newsgroup is much the same as posting an email. Again, if you want to know more, check out **The Virgin Guide to the Internet**.

Remember that newsgroups are volatile beasts. People can and will say anything, as well as send messages with all manner of vile or pornographic attachments. There is no control. If you have children, keep them away from them, and yourself too if you're of a sensitive disposition. If, though, you like to speak your mind and don't mind having your notions challenged, if you're prepared for the juiciest of gossip and most blasphemous of rumours (and, of course, if you're looking for info you won't find elsewhere), check out the examples below. For some of you, that will be enough, thank you very much. Others will never be heard of again. And all because they were looking for hidden meanings behind Radiohead's 'Creep'. What a waste! Good luck.

//ADDRESS BOOK

Portals/Search Engines

The All Music Guide   http://www.allmusic.com

Simply the best artist search guide. It is well written, concise and across the board – type in any band name to find biogs, articles and quality photos. It represents the combined toils of over 200 experienced writers and you will find it used on dozens of lesser sites, credited as AMG.

AltaVista   http://dir.altavista.com/Arts/Music.shtml

The musicky bit of this search engine is the one many experts recommend. There isn't much content but, as long as you have the Boolean basics of how to work the search field, you're laughing all the way to the site.

Clickmusic   http://www.clickmusic.co.uk

Call us biased, but this really is a fine site. Much more than the portal it is intended to be, it also offers news updated every five minutes, celebrity columns on music/net issues, and an amusing games section. Each category, whether it is an artist or a shop you seek, has its own individual guide, which advises you – like this book – on the best of what is out there. Bookmark away.

Excite!   http://nt.excite.com/142/music

Not really much music content, but this portal is a good search tool for the web and appears to have a frequently updated music database with few links that don't work.

Google   http://www.google.com

A fantastic search engine, fast, simple and original. It offers 'GoogleScout', a tool that searches around the site you have chosen to find a company's competitors plus the 'I'm Feeling Lucky' button, which takes you directly to the first site on the search list. This is a great idea because, as Google say 'it means less time searching for web pages and more time looking at them'.

Infoseek   http://infoseek.go.com/Topic/Music?tid=242
Part of the Go Network, this portal lists each music site with icons denoting whether there is MP3, audio stream, and other useful info.

Launch   http://www.launch.com
It's a search engine, it's a store, it's a webzine, it's a video channel. Blimey! They also believe that, despite the sound and visual quality not being as good as MTV, the fact that you can watch whatever you want when you want is their key to becoming the video channel of the future.

Northern Light   http://www.northernlight.com
A search engine recommended by those in the business. Fast and efficient, it doesn't show off with content, just finding you the music.

Yahoo!   http://uk.news.yahoo.com/m/music.html
A portal that gets most of its content from Virgin Net. Reviews, features, news, and a really fast search engine. For US visitors and for slightly more content try http://rock.yahoo.com.

Metasearchers

AskJeeves   http://www.askjeeves.com
Some might call this a search assistant, but what the hell! Phrase your question as if you were asking the butler to get you something – none of this Boolean 'OR' business with meta-type searchers. Your search becomes much more extensive and,

hopefully, accurate. We were given so many suggestions for London clubs that we ended up staying in.

Metacrawler   http://www.metacrawler.com
Another excellent metasearch engine. You need to be precise with your requests (i.e. use 'OR' when relevant), but it is very fast and accurate. Recommended.

DogPile   http://www.dogpile.com
Legendary, and pretty effective.

Music Databases

A Pop Music Directory   http://www.pop-music.com
Not limited to pop – although very good at it – this site also has a fairly good dance music directory and is currently building a rock and indie database. The news is fed from various sources, e.g. http://www.bbcamerica.com, and is updated daily. Look out for their sections on bands like Steps, Aqua and B*witched.

About.Com   http://home.about.com/entertainment
The site that promises experts on every subject you could possibly think of offers an exhaustive and exhausting directory of music categories, from alternative to world via home recording and MP3. Sections we checked out were well written and informed, offering thousands of links to relevant sites. There is even a Beatles category, which attempts to document every Beatles site currently on the web. Haven't they got homes to go to?

Amazon   http://www.amazon.com/music
A store site that acts like a reference database: classical and popular artists are catalogued, albums are recommended by reliable writers, and there are free downloads. Also, try

http://www.amazon.co.uk/music if you live in the UK and want to read reviews by UK customers – a good way of getting to the truth if ever there was one. It is out there, you know.

Artist Direct Network – The Ultimate Band List   http://ubl.com
This site is so much more than just an online store that it warrants a mention as a good starter site too: up-to-date news, features, links and audio clips. Oh, and detailed information, courtesy of those nice All Music Guide people.

BBC Pop   http://www.bbc.co.uk/entertainment/popmusic
A good start for anyone new to the web is the massive number of helpful BBC sites; this one is a general pop music one with a broad sweep of news, features and links to the more specific BBC sites associated with programmes such as Later and Top of the Pops, and the excellent Radio 1.

Change Music.Com   http://www.changemusic.com
Change Music – now merged with CMJ, one of the United States' most respected alternative-music information companies – is designed to maximise any search for a label, artist or music-related company. A good industry tool for bands, particularly those in the US.

Charts All Over The World   http://www.lanet.lv/misc/charts/
Not just top of the British pops or the Billboard 100, but who is selling in Latvia, Lithuania or the Cayman Islands. Updated weekly, it's a feast of anorak fun!

Indie World –   http://www.headspace.org
The Supersonic Guide   /iworld/supersonic/
Don't be fooled by the terrible, dated Britpop-style graphics – this will narrow your search for indie stuff down considerably, whether it's shoegazing, bigbeat or crybaby-rock.

Music 365   http://www.music365.co.uk
Midway between the NME online magazine and a more US-style
information-cum-shopping-mall site, Music 365 is a tremendous
place to go for news and reviews of contemporary music events.
The irreverent sense of humour is most welcome, particularly when
it comes to live interviews when the fans get involved. Check out
the archived mega-chats now. The one with Duran Duran's Simon
LeBon is something special.

Music Station   http://www.musicstation.com/musicnewswire
This provides the most up-to-date music news you'll find
anywhere. It's very much a 'global guide' with industry stories,
features and reviews, plus links to the news sources and the online
store CD Now, and, most recently, MP3 links.

Muze.com   http://www.muze.com
Rock, pop, jazz, classical, opera, an encyclopedia of music, the Top
100 albums ... this thing is bloody enormous!

Radio 1   http://www.bbc.co.uk/radio1
Excellent across-the-board pop coverage and a must for any
information hunter keen to find out what is going on in the UK
music world. It's particularly strong on indie music because of
Lamacq's Evening Session.

Rough Guide To Rock   http://www.roughguides.com/rock
Now the whole Rough Guide To Rock A-Z is online, rather than the
brief snippets they used to give us. The writing is, on the whole, of
a good standard. The only irritation is the occasional inexplicable
absence of important artists and the inclusion of too many early
90s non-entities.

SonicNet   http://www.sonicnet.com/front/index.jhtml
A very fast database search for any artist, however obscure. We

asked for some unusual names and received biographies, discographies, photos and links taking us to purchase points. You will also find news and great links to the MTV and VH1 net channels and loads of net radio links.

Tunes.com   **http://www.tunes.com/home**
Loads of news, MP3s videos and audio streaming and biographies from those AMG folk again – a good-looking one-stop destination for all things music. Try also the related Jam TV at **http://jamtv. tunes.com**.

Virgin   **http://www.virgin.net/music/index.html**
The homepage for UK Virgin's ISP is available to all, and very good it is too: a gig guide, well-written features, reviews and, of course, news. For UK visitors, it is very easy to find out what you are looking for. There are loads of competitions and special offers too.

Newsgroups

Remember, newsgroups are grouped into (pretty wide) categories, and the first few letters of each title tell you the score. For example, 'alt' means alternative, so you might be involving yourself is something chaotic, rude or groovy, while 'rec' means recreation, such as sports, etc. Really, you're going to love it.

alt.music.abba
Argue about the B-sides.

alt.music.techno
From Teutonic trance to nosebleed, this newsgroup attracts them all.

alt.music.syd-barret
Still the most talked-about 60s casualty.

rec.music.makers.bagpipes
Read about it without having to listen.

rec.music.marketplace
Anyone got any Shamen?

rec.music.songwriting
You're not alone.

uk.music.alternative
Still one of the most popular discussion forums.

4// I HEARD THE NEWS TODAY, OH BOY

Music is clearly ideally suited to the Internet's new systems of communication. And, whether they be considered music's champions, companions or parasites, music magazines have made great efforts to keep abreast of new developments. Most traditional magazines now concentrate heavily on their websites, meaning there are now hundreds of good-quality webzines to choose from. Some have even rejected the old ways of paper and ink entirely and turned themselves into net-only ventures.

The reasons for this are legion, and many are financial. Putting a magazine directly on to the web clearly saves you buying tons of paper, printing up thousands of issues, then transporting them all over the planet – only to have half of them returned unbought. Cutting such costs would be an attractive proposition for any business, and particularly one struggling in a marketplace as overpopulated as that of magazines.

Perhaps the most important advantage of web-based mags is that they are so organic. Research has consistently shown that most readers of music magazines turn first to the news section, then the letters pages, then to reviews – they like to stay on top of current events and opinions. A net magazine can easily update each of these sections every day, even every few minutes, whereas monthly land-based mags like Rolling Stone (http://www.rollingstone.com), Spin (http://www.spin.com) or Q (http://www.qonline.co.uk) require between one and two weeks for printing and distribution once an issue has been 'wrapped up'. Even weekly mags like NME (http://www.nme.com) may end up sitting on a story for seven days before its next issue hits the streets. It's said that 15 minutes is a long time in pop, and net mags clearly have the edge when it comes to speed of reaction.

Fans and the proprietors of land-based music magazines believe they will survive. It's that tactile thing: people like to possess objects, to hold their reading matter in their hands. They like to dip into magazines in those dead moments – on the train, at the bus stop, when the boss is out of the office. That's why they favour the shorter pieces mentioned above. Magazines have their own styles and attitudes and histories, and people react well to that: it gives them a sense of belonging. Or so it's claimed. The argument does sound horribly like the ones lovers of vinyl used to dismiss the chances of the CD format – people like to feel their records, they like to study the artwork etc. etc. The fact of the matter is that the sales of virtually all land-based music mags continue to fall, and many keep their figures artificially high by giving away free CDs they pray will be paid for by extra advertising revenue.

Since the US magazine *Addicted To Noise* (**http://www. addict.com**) took up the cyber-gauntlet back in 1995, the advances made by web mags have been huge. As said, all the major music mags now have effective websites, and most have now recognised the constrictions and advantages of the new technologies. Most obviously, they can put their own long-forgotten back issues to use again, putting up all those old features and reviews (in some cases reaching back over 50 years) and turning themselves into fascinating music archives. A net feature can be stored and easily accessed for ever. A magazine, as the saying goes, is only tomorrow's fish-and-chip paper.

What webzines are like

On first visiting a web magazine, you'll probably be surprised by the sheer weight of information on the homepage. The first few spreads of a paper-based mag will consist of adverts, various contents pages, an editorial message and probably a letters page, all leading you gently into the issue. But a web mag, as speed and convenience are of the essence for new and regular visitors alike, will usually cram news, links, everything on to its first page – that generally being a vertical spread that you'll spend some time scrolling down.

Addicted To Noise, for instance, offers a different set of CD reviews every day, continually updated news, videos on demand and an easily accessible and alphabetically ordered archive of hundreds of features stretching back to 1995. The features are excellent – well considered, well written and sometimes lasting over a gratifying eight or nine pages – and take in contemporary US faves like Ani DiFranco, Phish and Limp Bizkit, as well as Brit hipsters like Portishead, Radiohead and Spiritualized. You'll also find more general pieces on writers like Greil Marcus, Charles Bukowski and William Gibson, as well as still-compelling old-school rockers like John Fogerty and Tom Waits. Beside each feature will be buttons allowing you to download 45-second excerpts from the interviewee's tracks (in stereo or mono MP3 or RealAudio), or buy them. You can furthermore watch video interviews via a link to SonicNet.

As you'd expect, each web mag battles to seem the most on the ball and active, and most of the major players have something to offer. The straight-faced NME is the Mecca for indie fans, but also provides excellent reviews, 20 years of classic rock quotes, good links, allows you to chat to bands and send your friends a postcard featuring a famous NME cover and, best of all, possesses a music directory for all your needs – whether you're seeking a school, a teacher, hi-fi, instruments, or CD retailers and manufacturers.

The daddy of them all though is *Rolling Stone*. This mag's cultural status and massive subscription sales have made it steady and rich enough to pump major resources into its site. Thus *Rolling Stone's* homepage is an eye-boggling mass of detail – there's not even enough room for the kind of flashing adverts (Nike and the Honda Civic Hatchback are commonplace) that spoil the look of the competition. There's an encyclopedic Artist A-Z, news, current features, reviews, games, contests, and photo archives. You can watch videos, and special made-for-online video interviews, buy CDs (via a link to CD Now) and the merchandise of many major acts and, if you're American, check what's on in your local city. New acts are invited to send in MP3s, the ten best of which are made available for download every two weeks. And, being the name in rock mags, they can offer frequent webcasts of exceptional quality, one fairly typical week featuring David Bowie, Cypress Hill, Culture Club, Eminem and Bo Bud Greene.

Here's how deep Rolling Stone is: if you go far, far in to the Tom Waits pages, you'll find a 'Trivia' section within the 'Trivia' section. It's so trivial, the readers set the questions, then sit back and laugh uproariously as the printed percentage of wrong answers steadily rises. Awesome stuff.

Many feared that, with rock stars now treated as 'celebrities' and music-based articles now appearing in every tabloid and magazine on the shelves, specialist music mags would have nothing different to offer, and would thus die. The Internet, though, seems to have saved them. The MP3 revolution, which has made millions of tracks by hundreds of thousands of bands available, makes their job of ordering, describing, filtering and recommending all the more vital. The chance to archive old issues lends them scope and gravitas. Chat rooms and message boards bring their readers together as a like-minded (sometimes vociferously varied) community. And, of course, this technology allows mags to take their readers right into the heart of the action, with live concerts and live interviews in which you get to ask the questions – how refreshing is that?

Magazines

Addicted To Noise   http://www.addict.com
Very simple idea – interviews by knowledgeable US journalists. Archives go back to 1995.

Billboard   http://www.billboard.com
Up-to-date, on-the-mark US music-biz news, plus all the definitive US charts and the Holy Grail itself: the Billboard Hot 100 singles.

Blah 3.Com   http://www.rantuk.com
A UK music news site with a detailed focus on alternative bands. Sharp reviews are backed up with lots of Real Audio clips.

Bunnyhop   http://www.bunnyhop.com
A great US slacker monthly magazine, packed with irony and self-deprecation. Lots of interviews with US alternative bands.

Country Cool.Co   http://www.countrycool.com
It's billed as the World of Country Music, and there is nothing you need worry about missing once you're here. All the new releases are reviewed, all the brightest stars interviewed.

Crawdaddy   http://www.cdaddy.com

A web version of the long-established US classic-rock magazine. A library of informed Mojo-style interviews and features.

Dazed And Confused   http://www.confused.com

Some good photographs by Rankin, owner of this UK fashion/ music mag, which has allegedly superseded The Face. Too much earnest text for some tastes. The A-Z of Pleasure is fun, though.

Dotmusic   http://www.dotmusic.co.uk

A so-called insider's guide but with teen-pop style graphics and editorial style. The news is always up to date and the dance section is especially in-depth and readable.

DownBeat   http://downbeatjazz.tunes.com

Wise, thoughtful jazz writing from the famous US magazine, with a solid news section and plenty of features and archives to choose from. Nice.

Loaded   http://www.uploaded.com

Not exclusively a music magazine, but written amusingly by those informed by the UK music scene; an offensive load of sexist nonsense or an inspired original, depending on your sensibilities.

Mad as a Fish   http://www.madsasafish.com

Well-written reviews from this amusingly titled MP3-orientated UK shop site. Frequently updated news and features are augmented by a great 'Music on TV and Radio' section. And fish.

Mixmag/Mixmag Update   http://www.techno.de/mixmag

Germany, the world's techno music Zentrum, provides the site for this UK DJ magazine. It's definitive in its white-label/promo chart and informative in the news section for DJs and clubbers alike. But, like a coked-up raver at six in the morning, it just looks awful.

MTV   http://www.mtv.com

A vicious assault on the eyes but promising much. This site perhaps doesn't give us the instant thrill of the channel but it's only a matter of time. The current '100 Best Videos' feature is great for streaming your fave clips.

Music 365   http://www.music365.co.uk

News stories lead on this site, backed up with informed and sometimes hilarious reviews, features and shopping facilities. Have a look at the 'Community' section for a great letters page.

NME   http://www.nme.com

Wretched-looking, but content- and attitude-rich. One of the best contemporary, Brit-orientated music news sites. As well as Features, webcasts and a controversial chat/letters page, it also boasts an informed archive of reviews going back to those heady Madchester nights of 1990.

Q   http://www.qonline.co.uk

Clear and concise news and reviews credited to reputable, grown-up writers, with an archive dating right back to when Q was a baby. The Q-Studio promises the thrill of being a producer but unfortunately, like many producers, doesn't appear to work.

Rolling Stone   http://www.rollingstone.com

The mother of all music magazines has a baby. The meat of news is down the spine of the main page flanked by hot clicks, directories, and a fantastic artist index.

Rootsworld   http://www.rootsworld.com

The latest news and a superb archive of reviews on world music from Africa to Europe to the Pacific Rim; from ska to bagpipes. Also, it's surprisingly easy to find your way around with the useful search field.

Sleazenation   http://www.sleazenation.com
Alternative rock, UK style with well-written pieces by those who
know. Just watch out the graphics don't crash your PC.

Sonicnet Online Music Network   http://www.sonicnet.com
This US-centric music site is all-encompassing, with as many MP3s
and Real Audio feeds as daily updated news and review items.
Particularly fascinating is its weekly 'Development of Music in
Cyberspace' feature. The future.

Spin   http://www.spin.com
All the news, interviews and webcasts you would expect from
the online sister of the cool US alternative rock mag, with an
archive of the current year's features. Perhaps a little too earnest
for its own good.

The Source   http://www.thesource.com
Everything you want to know about hip-hop, updated daily.

The Wire   http://www.dfuse.com
Disappointing site from the impressive new-music magazine. A few
archived features but essentially a virtual carrot persuading us to
take out a subscription.

The Last Resort http://members.aol.com/surfsean/TLR/index.htm
Amateurish but informative UK music news site, providing useful
links and often useless interviews.

This is London   http://www.thisislondon.co.uk
London's Evening Standard online. A great guide to the dirty city and
very useful for those interested in 'avin' it large in a club or at a gig.

Time Out   http://www.timeout.com
A bit scant compared with the excellent what's-on magazine that
now covers New York as well as London. This is perhaps because

virtually every other world capital is featured here too. Good for clubbing around the globe.

Top http://www.topmag.co.uk
Tower Records' free magazine's UK site, with daily updated news plus features and reviews.

Top of the Pops http://www.totp.beeb.com
Like the magazine: packed with all the current chart favourites, with news, useful links and competitions.

Virgin.Net http://www.virgin.net
At the risk of appearing biased, I have to say that this really is a homepage with an exceptionally fine music content. The latest news from NME and other news specialists comes in hourly updated packages, the reviews are well written and there is an 'Upcoming CD Release' section.

Wall of Sound http://wallofsound.go.com
A US-based e-zine with a comprehensive and succinct selection of news, reviews, features, plus the definitive Billboard Charts.

Yahoo! Music UK & http://uk.news.yahoo.com/m/music.html
Ireland
A homepage not dissimilar to Virgin's – indeed featuring some of the same writers – but not quite as on the mark for news. Very good for music links, of course.

5//5-4-3-2-1 ... MELTDOWN!

It's widely believed that the onset of the Internet era will result in an apocalyptic meltdown of the music industry. It's said that record companies and high-street retailers have colluded in keeping CD prices artificially high and will consequently suffer a fatal drop in revenue as music lovers take advantage of the cheap deals offered by web-based super-retailers like CD Now and CD Universe.

Beyond this, it's claimed (not least by Prince and George Michael) that record companies have hitherto kept their artists in 'slavery' – controlling their artistic output and extorting vast percentages of their income – and will lose their hold now that MP3 and other digital audio formats allow consumers to download music direct from the musician's own site. Record companies, then, have become unnecessary middlemen and are thus doomed to die. Or so it's said ...

The future of record companies
While it's certainly true that web trading has increased overall music sales, high-street retailers may well find their trade gradually dropping off, driving them towards less traditional methods of selling. Record companies, though – canny and adaptable as ever – are unlikely to relinquish their pre-eminence.

Money is a vital factor. Major labels are able to offer musicians large advances enabling them to concentrate full-time on music, and record their tracks in the way they'd like – hiring producers, mixers and full orchestras can be extremely expensive. Furthermore, their financial muscle allows them to advertise musicians' wares widely both on the Internet and in the printed press, as well as hire radio pluggers, press officers and merchandisers. They can provide a tour budget too.

Aside from finance, record companies can also offer to acts their industry experience, marketing expertise and helpful contacts with managers, booking agents, publishers, studios, producers, caterers, limo firms and even other band members. While it's true that musicians can now upload their material and sell direct to consumers, keeping all profits and rights for themselves, savage competition between the (literally) hundreds of thousands of acts out there means that making a life-sustaining profit, let alone achieving stardom, usually requires more. Of course, labels can offer no guarantee, and are famously money-minded (like any other big business), but can provide musicians with services they should not and will not blindly ignore.

Already, record companies, rather than succumbing to the power of the web, have begun to use it to their best advantage, promoting their acts and selling their products. Such major acts as Tori Amos, Puff Daddy, TLC and Sebadoh have all had tracks made available exclusively to Internet users as tasters to publicise forth-coming albums. Labels have also begun to make tracks available in highly sophisticated digital formats like Liquid Audio and Microsoft's Windows Media Audio, which allow files to self-destruct after a specific period if the customer fails to pay the fee for downloading (see Chapter 1, 'The Revolution is Here').

On top of this, the vast and ever-increasing back catalogue of music owned by record companies is now being made available, again via Liquid Audio and its like. Thus all their material – catalogues in some cases reaching back to the beginning of the 1900s – will be available for purchase at all times. There need be no deletions, and no shoddy reprints – a blessing for all music lovers.

What you see and what you get

As far as their official sites went, record companies were slow to explore the Internet's myriad possibilities. Most were unimaginative, even shoddy, dedicated solely to selling rather than entertainment and intrigue. You'd often be confronted with a dull front page leading you to artist pages offering bland photos and only cursory news information.

But this is changing as the industry catches on – and it's catching on fast, as the merging of AOL, Time-Warner and EMI conclusively proved. Nowadays, label sites are deeper, more professionally constructed and far more useful and entertaining. Columbia (http://www.columbiarecords.com), for instance, though still far from the cutting edge, do at least now offer release schedules, gig listings and up-to-date news, as well as concise biographies and sharp pix of all their artists. You can hear tracks and watch full-length videos. There are also guides to associated labels like American, Loud and So So Def, a guide to the best independent stores in the US (amazing for a major label) and, probably best of all, a guide to the enormous back catalogue of their parent company Sony – which stretches from the ultra-contemporary Fiona Apple, through Argent and Julie Andrews to the Abyssinian Baptist Gospel Choir.

Of course, there's also a store, where you can purchase DVDs, videos, CDs, tapes, vinyl, minidiscs and even sheet music showing you how to play the hits of Bob Dylan on harmonica. And, for those keen to make Columbia compilations, there's a link to the excellent Musicmaker.com.

Some label sites pride themselves on being a little more cutting-edge. Madonna's Maverick label (http://www.maverickrc.com), for instance, immediately suggests you install Flash 3 – offered free of charge – so you can fully appreciate their lovingly animated graphics. Artist pages are cool and no-nonsense – the Prodigy's, at the time of writing, simply features a logo and the terse message 'We Will Be Back' – and there are extremely busy fan forums where crazily hopeful men claim that 'I am going to marry Madonna very soon' and forceful women use language not often seen outside the works of Henry Miller.

Major-label sites can often be annoyingly self-congratulatory, constantly hammering you with sales statistics or news of their latest Grammy nomination. But this is the nature of the corporate beast. For those preferring a more personal touch, there are also links to sites run by the artists themselves.

//ADDRESS BOOK

Major Labels

BMG

Arista US   http://www.aristarec.com
Good-looking and fun to use. Arista manage to fuse content from the Grateful Dead, TLC, Barry Manilow and the Partridge Family and still have an identity.

BMG UK Backstage   http://www.bmg.co.uk
Infuriating. Akin to Fort Knox in accessibility and then – once you're inside – difficult to navigate as well. We registered and asked to see some Elvis stuff: nothing doing – we were led directly to the News Page and then couldn't escape. No Presley news either because he's been dead for years. Looks dated too – the site, that is, not the King.

BMG US   http://www.bmg.com

The US umbrella site for RCA, Arista, BMG Classics and other related labels is intentionally and frighteningly corporate but does lead to the friendlier link http://www.peeps.com, Arista's own site and the corporation's own online store http://www.getmusic.com.

Jive   http://www.peeps.com/jiverecords/index.html

Home to acts like R Kelly and Steps, this is so well organised and nicely turned out that you could take it home to meet your mum.

RCA US   http://www.peeps.com/artists/frames/rca.html

A simple index of the US labels roster. There seems to be no other content but Peeps.com is useful to scour BMG's roster in the US.

EMI/Virgin

Capitol Records   http://www.hollywoodandvine.com

One of the smartest major-label sites not least because of its impressive roster (Beastie Boys, Beatles, Robbie Williams, etc.) the latest news, tour dates and artist information – a great 'Easy Listening' section too.

EMI-Chrysalis   http://www.emirecords.co.uk

Badly designed, trying to cover all the disparate musical bases. Identity- and attitude-free, in the way only major corporations know how to be.

Food Records   http://www.foodrecords.co.uk

Chalked graphics and a 'street' look suggest major-label nonsense, but this is fabulous, well written and informative. Features include a year-by-year history of the label, a brilliant up-to-date news section, and a chat room. They even tell us about new signings before release.

Parlophone   http://www.lookon.net
Blur, Beastie Boys, Radiohead and Supergrass, loads of audio
streams – often from forthcoming releases – and a 'Make your own
video' feature. How long will this fantastic site last, now that EMI is
no longer a standalone company?

Virgin UK site   http://www.vmg.co.uk
The UK site splits the company into useful genre-based labels, each
of which has a section: 'The Raft' specialises in the indie genre with
labels like Hut, the Verve, Smashing Pumpkins, Air etc.; 'C3'
features pop artists like Billie and the Spice Girls; and 'EDEN', the
more adult-orientated site, has the Rolling Stones and George
Michael.

Virgin Records Pop Site – C3   http://www.c3.vmg.co.uk
Including all Virgin's current money-spinners; news is constantly
updated and the exclusives are great – check out the footage of
Billie being dropped by one of her dancers. Because they want to.

Virgin Records – The Raft   http://www.theraft.com
Virgin's specialist alternative site doesn't need to do much more
than provide links to the artists on its impressive roster, but it
somehow manages to do just that, like giving us a sneaky peek at
forthcoming unreleased tracks.

Virgin US   http://www.virginrecords.com
Blessed with a roster from Bowie to the Chemical Brothers to the
Smashing Pumpkins, Virgin have maximised the potential and
given us something good-looking and easily navigable.

Polygram/Universal

Almo   http://www.almosounds.com/
This takes a while to load up, but when it has finally reached the

screen we have access to quality artists like the label boss Herb Alpert and the goth-moaners Garbage.

Blue Note   http://www.bluenote.com
From the label perhaps most famous for Reed Miles's innovative sleeve design, this is unsurprisingly cool-looking. Even if you can't quite remember how to spell Herbie Hancock, the search facility makes it possible to scan the whole catalogue. There's also up-to-date news, interviews, tour dates and selected RealAudio streams in the Jukebox section. Great.

Interscope   http://www.interscoperecords.com
Limp Bizkit, Dr Dre, Sherryl Crow, Counting Crows and Beck; this label has a fine roster and, unlike a lot of the Seagrams-owned labels, has escaped the fate of having a terrible or non-existent website. The graphics are impressive, the navigation easy and clear, and each artist's news page is constantly updated. Very sexy.

Island   http://www.island.co.uk
Despite cool visuals of a local record store walk-through, the home of Pulp, Bob Marley and Tricky feels old-fashioned and neglected – perhaps because Island's ownership has changed. The tour and release news is several months old and there are no links to other sites.

Island Def Jam   http://www.islanddefjam.com
Oh, this major label meltdown has really thrown the website world into confusion! Part of this site was once the Mercury Records site, so we now get Elvis Costello crouching uncomfortably next to LL Cool J and Dru Hill. Once an artist's page has been reached we discover that is exactly what it is: one page of text with no links. A stopgap site, surely.

MCA Records America http://www.mcarecords.com

From Aqua to Semisonic, with frequent nods towards country music, MCA seem to be keeping their identity successfully via their online presence.

Polydor http://www.polydor.co.uk

The homepage looks like a cool venue and promises much, but once you get inside you have to register with your email address, which is time-consuming and ultimately not worth the effort since each band on the label has its own, much better, site.

Universal Music http://www.universalmusic.com

Alfred Hitchcock's image springs up, followed by Sting's. Hmm. Once the screen is filled, it's an uninspiring blend of heavyweight and new artists. The links are good, though.

Universal Classics http://www.universalclassics.com

Giving you access to the rosters of the classical labels Deutsche Grammophon, Philips and Decca, this is content-rich, but, needless to say, geared towards making us shell out as quick as possible. Each artist has a biography and some pictures – but wouldn't it be more useful to have a search system by composer?

Verve http://www.vervemusicgroup.com/
Records verve/index.html

All the greats like Ella, Duke, Oscar Peterson, Stan Getz, Sonny Rollins plus contemporaries like Mark Antoine and Al Jarreau – this is a good place to visit due to its tear-jerkingly good roster.

Sony

Columbia http://www.columbiarecords.com

Old-fashioned-looking but fairly comprehensive from a label with a once-fabulous roster. The forthcoming-release section is just a typed-up list on a sheet of A4, and the new-artist sections are a genre-jumbled mess. There's a lot of info here, though.

Ruffhouse http://www.ruffhouse.com
Columbia Records' urban label offers a directory of the artists on the label – no mucking about here, just links to talent such as Lauryn Hill and Cyprus Hill.

Sony US http://www.sonymusic.com
A more 'street' look. Graffiti-style stencilled graphics and bold brushstrokes disguise limited content. Destinations like 'Artists', 'Music', 'The Lab' and so on lead to pretty much the same thing – a field where you may type in your favourite artist.

Sony UK http://www.sonymusic.co.uk
No-nonsense, easy to use and good-looking – pack shots of clickable forthcoming releases and news in the middle with an index of the whole roster in the left-hand column.

Warners/WEA

Atlantic http://www.atlantic-records.com
Anyone expecting a fabulous trawl through the fifties jazz of Ray Charles and the 60s triumphs of soul and R&B stars like Aretha and Otis will be left disappointed by visiting this average site from the former Ahmet Ertegun/Jerry Wexler label.

East West Records http://www.eastwest.co.uk
Unavailable at the time of writing, but will be up and running shortly (maybe by the time you read this), giving you the official lowdown on the those curly-headed sexpots Tori Amos and Mick Hucknall.

Maverick http://www.maverickrc.com/
Unsurprisingly, Madonna's label manages to achieve an individual

style like no other. There are forums on each act, and links to the now impressive roster, which includes Alanis Morrissette and soundtracks to movies such as Austin Powers – type a slash after the address and the project you want

Reprise   http://www.RepriseRec.com
Lovingly put together and taking pride in the fact that Neil Young has re-signed to the label after 25 years. The news section is excellent, there are QuickTime videos to view, and the overall feel and look is fabulous. Add a slash after the address, then the name of your chosen artist.

Warner Brothers Records USA   http://www.wbr.com
Like a bad holiday destination, this US site is dull and takes ages to get to. Corporate shields appear mounted on a black wall, each one representing an artist or a movie – the artists are the newer ones like Faith Hill and Paula Cole, rather than Joni or REM.

Warner Brothers Online   http://www.music.warnerbros.com/
More shields for bigger artists (Clapton) plus labels like Rhino and Atlantic. The ubiquitous Paula Cole crops up again.

WEA Records UK   http://www.wea.co.uk
Unavailable at the time of writing, but will be doubtless shortly be striking against its corporate reputation and testing the boundaries of artistic achievement.

Independent Labels

3MV

The Knowledge   http://www.theknowledge.com
From the indie distributor 3MV, this is a fantastic selection of indie and mainstream labels with audio, video, biogs and gigs info. Recommended.

Ace   http://www.acerecords.co.uk

Home to an impressive selection of re-release labels like Big Beat, Kent, Stax and Prestige. Sadly, all we have here is a list of the label's – admittedly fine – catalogue of rock 'n' roll to funk to punk, but no audio stream, biogs or news.

Beggars Banquet   http://www.beggars.com

A homepage for Beggars and all its associated labels; Mantra, Wiija, Mowax, 4AD, Too Pure and XL. Very artist-based, since the labels, being cool and image-rich to begin with, have little to prove.

Deceptive   http://www.deceptive.co.uk

The indie, famed for bringing us Elastica, has embraced the web with a zealous pride and is now proclaiming the release of the first ever email single. Artists such as Snuff and Superfine get clear and up-to-date news items and the artists among us are welcome to send our demos in.

Domino Records   http://www.dominorecordco.com

The UK label that largely specialises in US alternative bands such as the Sebadoh, Pavement, the Palace Brothers and Mouse On Mars offers a friendly, easy-to-use site. It doesn't try too hard to impress us with flashy hi-tech graphics, just gives us the artists, the merch, and the inside info.

Chemikal Underground   http://www.chemikal.demon.co.uk

Find out about acts such as Mogwai, Cha Cha Cohen and the Delgados with one of the most important indie labels. There is a front page containing label news too.

Cooking Vinyl   http://www.cookingvinyl.com

Making the most of their interesting and eclectic folk-ish roster (XTC, the Lilac Time, Violent Femmes, Ani DiFranco, Wedding Present etc.), they give each artist a detailed personal page.

ECM   http://www.ecmrecords.com

Manfrid Eicher's Munich-based ambient and jazz label, formed in 1969, offers an impressive web presence, with definitive biographies of all the artists from Jan Garbarek to Robert Wyatt.

Edel   http://www.edel.co.uk

The German company who own Vital distribution and Play It Again Sam, home to masses of cool indie labels.

Epitaph   http://www.epitaph.com

Not a pretty site (ho ho ho), but practical and packed, from the US rock label made rich and famous by the Offspring.

Hyperion   http://www.hyperion-records.co.uk

Award-winning British classical-music label produces a website of an equally fine quality: search by artist or composer and hear the superb range of recordings in Real Audio sample. This really is how all classical labels should be – there's even a huge article on why CDs cost what they do.

Jeepster   http://www.jeepster.com

A good start if you are keen on the new Scottish scene that revolves around members of this label's number-one band Belle and Sebastian.

Matador Records   http://www.matador.recs.com

Hugely fashionable US college rock label covering acts from Yo La Tengo to Belle and Sebastian to Cornelius – the news is stylishly written and bang up to date, and the links to all the artists are easy to access. There is also tons of stuff from the in-house magazine, ¡Escandalo!, to read. Check out the how to write your own record review or feature at **http://www2.matador.recs.com/mata/diy/diy.html**. Great!

Motown   http://www.motown.com

This site was still under construction at the time of writing. If it is at the time of reading, you can link to Motown artist sites via the Smokey Robinson fan club page at http://www3.edgenet.net/smokey_miracles.

Mo'Wax   http://www.mowax.com

If you have Flash, you'll find that this is one of the most visually beautiful sites around – a testament to the large sums cash that the now impotent A&M indulged in the label and the UNKLE project. There is virtually nothing to read, just lots of sexy graphics dancing before your eyes as you hear audio streams and exclusive tracks. The games are fun too.

Mute   http://www.mutelibtech.com/mute

Daniel Miller's label is still idiosyncratic and appealing despite major mainstream success with Depeche Mode and Erasure. Here at Mute Liberation Technology, music and information rule over aesthetics, which suits the label's minimalist style. News is bang up to date and each artist is given an individual site with links to others. There are some audio clips on the front page.

Naxos   http://www.hnh.com

These are the people who brought cheap classical music to the masses, annoying the purists with their 'Best Of' collections but proving an absolute godsend to the rest of us. There is also a UK version of this excellent homepage.

Nimbus   http://www.nimbus.ltd.uk/nrl/index.html

Great classical label matching its quality online.

Ninja Tunes   http://www.ninjatune.com

The Coldcut supremos – for Ninja is their label – famously relish technology as much as they do music. As well as the latter in

Real Audio form, this superb, constantly updated and obsessive site has exclusive cartoons and games, plus links to many other great dance locations.

Nude   http://www.nuderecords.com
Stylish in the extreme, Nude boasts a Frank Lloyd Wright-style virtual building with all the usual links to artists, merchandise and stuff you need. Real Audio of all the artists, too, is a bonus, particularly Suede.

One Little Indian   http://www.indian.co.uk
Kicks off with all the news and the new releases. The label best known for Björk offers a stylish and functional place to find out about its artists.

Outcaste   http://www.outcaste.com
Up to date, good-looking and informative, from Nitin Sawney's label; check out some great screensavers.

Pinnacle   http://www.pinnacle-records.co.uk
Another indie distributor now with its own label – check out streamed audio, from Tom Waits to Groove Armada.

Rhino   http://www.rhino.com
Superb US reissue label; from the Monkees to Curtis Mayfield to 70s funk compilations and New York punk rock – all beautifully packaged, this matches the label's releases in style and wit, and gives you the opportunity to buy direct if you live in the US.

Roadrunner   http://www.roadrunnerrecords.com
Attitude and aggression from the company that brought us Sepultura and now Slipknot. This is a superb destination for all heavy-rock fans – with individual band pages, general label information, the lot.

Rykodisc

http://www.rykodisc.com

Brilliantly inspired; not only looks and feels good, but also delivers on content for each of its artists. The roster of this eclectic label comprises largely traditional rock figures such as Zappa, Robert Cray and Lloyd Cole, and movie soundtracks, but the presentation gives everything a relevant and contemporary feel. Real Audio clips of everything too.

Setanta

http://www.setantarecords.com

Functional rather than inspired from the label that gave you the Divine Comedy and Edwyn Collins – some good links, occasional competitions and the feel of real music fans putting it all together.

Skint

http://www.skint.net

Much more than just Fatboy Slim's record label, this is a fine example of a proper indie label wasting major label funds to have fun. All the favourites like Lo-Fidelity Allstars and Indian Ropeman etc. are biog-ed, discog-ed, and videog-ed with contributions from the label boss Damien Harris, and even a football page.

Subpop

http://www.subpop.com

The virtual home for the cool Seattle indie is self-deprecating and fun. Not only is there the expected list of artist pages, news and merchandise (the last of these excellent, as you might expect) but the links, such as http://www.sheeps.com, are inspired.

Telstar

http://www.telstar.co.uk/f_set.html

Boring corporate nonsense – is this really a record company?

V2

http://www.v2music.com

For a relatively new label this has all the look and feel of a veteran. Scroll down the list of artists to link to their homepage, check out links to the satellite labels all round the world or waste some time in the 'Remix' section.

Warp   **http://www.warpnet.com**

A good-looking 'We Are 10' site. The Sheffield label have made a lot of effort to celebrate the anniversary of their unique brand of leftfield dance – pages devoted to favourites such as Nightmares On Wax and LFO give way to exclusive screensavers and posters.

XL   **http://www.xl-recordings.com**

This offers Real Audio video streams of its artists as well as occasional flashes of inspiration like the 'Badly Drawn Boy' Story. The Prodigy site is a bit scant, as is the Basement Jaxx. Best to check out the sites mentioned elsewhere in this book.

6//FANS AND SUPERFANS

Conspiracy theorists, anarchists and even those who just like a good old barney will often harp on about how 'dangerous' the Internet is. The authorities hate it, e-fraud is rife, hackers are breaking into the Pentagon's computers and pointing nuclear missiles at Bethlehem! Holy Christ! Their point is basically that, as the saying goes, information is power. And the Net, being a so far uncontrolled source of information from anywhere and anyone, gives us power, liberates us, lets us say the unsayable and so on.

There is a truth to this – there's very little censorship on the web (though you might find yourself in trouble if you keep using the F-word in AOL's chat rooms for kids). On the Net, gems are uncovered and secrets revealed in every field, if you can be bothered to look. So violently has Net culture invaded the international consciousness that obsessives have started up sites about just about everything. All the obvious subjects are heavily covered – Charles Manson, the Roswell Incident, Jesus Our Lord. For a while back there, The X Files was so popular that Gillian Anderson (that's Agent Dana Scully to you) had more sites dedicated to her than anyone else on the planet. Kooky, huh?

Obsessions unleashed

And, of course, when it comes to obsessives, music has always had more than its fair share. Think Mark Chapman. Think about all the copycat suicides that followed the death of Kurt Cobain. Think of all the hunters and collectors who sleep in bus shelters as they pursue their idols across the planet, ever hopeful of securing a signed photo or, better still, a lock of hair to keep close to their hammering hearts. The world is full of them, and the Net is their spiritual home.

Back in the Bad Old Days, some five years back, obsessive fans could really only gaze from a distance. Getting backstage was as close as they could come to a band. And, for some of them, that wasn't enough. As 'true' fans who 'really cared' about their favourite bands, really wanted them to succeed, they needed to contribute and so published fanzines.

These were usually modelled on the likes of Sniffin' Glue, the punk fanzine launched by Mark Perry (later of the band ATV), and were really made possible by the spreading of punk's DIY ethic. Oh, and the availability of inexpensive photocopying. Fanzines were usually publishing catastrophes – eight pages of hopelessly subjective rantings, badly printed on the cheapest paper known to man. They'd be thrust into your hands at gigs by squat and serious toad-people, their bodies lost in voluminous camouflage jackets and their eyes peering out through three inches of cheaply horn-rimmed glass. For 50 pence you could share their massive intensity, and it was often worth it – they were so into it, the enthusiasm was infectious.

All of these people now run websites dedicated to their heroes. So do hundreds of thousands of more even-minded folk. Just as magazines have gleefully recognised that the Net negates paper costs and any need for postage or distribution, so have big fans, and sometimes simply those with a passing intellectual interest. To start up, all they need is an ISP (Internet Service Provider) to supply them with some web space, and away they go (see **The Virgin Guide to the Internet** for particulars on building your own site). Subject matter is down to them. Most concentrate on a single band; some prefer genres (for instance, mod or psychedelia); others go for decades (the 60s are big on the Net); some will rant on about absolutely anything. If you're lost for a place to start, try a general site such as Music Fan Clubs, or Fanclubs Database, which collects information on as many fan sites as it can and links to them.

Why fan sites rock
So what will you find on visiting a fan site? Well, dedication to duty, for one thing, and usually a charming sincerity severely lacking in most magazines. These people are expending their time and effort for no remuneration, and the care and attention obviously spent on the better sites (which often put official sites to shame) can be quite moving. They happily do their research, collect the best from international press files and other websites, and badger bands for information – upcoming tour dates and release schedules as well as more personal details, snippets of band history, the meaning of lyrics and lots of other stuff.

They'll often obtain much more information than more official sources as they'll put in more effort and hours, and bands tend to be fairly helpful as they're both pleased by the superfans' interest and guilt-tripped by their sacrifices. Some fascinating and quite embarrassing details can be turned up and published. The Net does bring editorial freedom. Fan sites, unlike magazines, do not rely for income on adverts from record companies, and so can afford to offend them. Obsessives, furthermore, are notoriously insensitive.

A further benefit provided by fan sites is a feeling of community. Previously, there were very few organised fan bases, where fans would contact each other, pass on information, rarities, live tapes or CDs, even organise conventions and days out. The Grateful Dead's followers, the Dead Heads, were probably the best known group, collating all information about the band and making available tapes of pretty much every one of the thousands of gigs they played. The same thing happened with the Dead soundalikes, Phish. The Internet has proliferated that feeling, and that kind of community. A really good fan site can tell you a great deal more than the company or band would have you know, and provide you with more recorded material than is perhaps legal. Most sites will positively welcome your input and opinions. E-buddies can be made very quickly indeed. Often disturbingly so.

Of course, many fan sites are dreadful, just the inconsequential mewlings of lovesick teenagers. They're characterised by jealousy, painful neediness and unselfconscious subjectivity. Their lack of professional editing can let major inaccuracies slip through. The term 'morbid interest' might have been invented for them. And they'll often spend inordinate amounts of time and space complaining bitterly about other sites dedicated to the same band. So much for community.

But, despite their evident drawbacks, fan sites are an important part of what the Internet, and music itself, are all about. They're volatile and independent-minded. Obsession can make them impressively informative and beautifully presented. They are often well tended and regularly updated (a tip: watch out for those addresses ending in 'edu'. These are based in US colleges and, though often quite brilliant, will tend to lie stagnant when school's out). Almost without exception, there will be a fan site somewhere that outshines every band's official site. Another tip: when using search engines to seek out good fan sites, remember that the engine's spiders will often be fooled into thinking a site is important or effective just by virtue of the fact that (a) it says it is and (b) it has copious mentions of a band's name. Those at the top of the search list can be among the scatterbrained worst.

Below is a list of some of the finest, featuring some of the world's biggest bands. Choose a band you know or like, try out the site (or sites) mentioned. Then follow the inevitable links to other fan sites dedicated to that band. Link again, and again. Go deeper and deeper, picking up all that information, misinformation and disinformation. Obsessives will always go further than you – that's why, at least as far as fan sites go, the Net never seems to end.

//ADDRESS BOOK

General Fan Sites

Anthems   http://www.anthems.com
News, tips, charts and pix all bound together in an engaging writing style, this is great UK dance music site for anyone even vaguely into 'avin' it.

Classical Music   http://www.richter.simplenet.com/
Index   music.html#pop
Absolutely brilliant fan page from one Paul, who gives us a description of his recommended links for composers. Packed.

Effectomatic Who   http://members.xoom.com/effectomatic
A site with real attitude. Kicking off with Oasis news, it goes on to rave about everyone from Bob Marley to Gay Dad. Useful links too.

Fansites Database   http://www.fansites.com
A large database for fan sites of all music types from reggae to new age.

Just The Music.com http://www.justthemusic.com
A US fan site dedicated to bringing the best new alternative music to people via weekly webcast. A great way of finding out about new artists, while also hearing the latest releases by more established favourites like Ben Folds Five and Lou Barlow.

The Mod Sixties http://www.realcrazy.freeserve.co.uk/
Web Ring mod-sixties-webring.htm
A UK hub site for a collection of passionate 60s music websites, with links to sites like Modern Schmodern, I Was Lord Kitchener's Valet, and the Official Aceface Homepage.

Music Fan Clubs http://www.musicfanclubs.org
Links to fan-club sites for a lot of quality artists – and a lot of terrible ones too, of course.

The Reggae Source http://www.reggaesource.com
Up to date and useful for reggae fans, this site is as good as a lot of flashier ones out there.

The Wonderwall http://www.beat.co.uk/wonderwall.html
Terrible-looking but useful site featuring UK and Irish indie bands. Includes a directory of record labels.

Yee Haw – The Official http://members.tripod.com/
I Hate Country Music Page ~Kalamazoo/
Inspired ranting about the much-maligned genre.

Artist-Specific Fan Sites

Abba http://www.danbbs.dk/~janbach/musikgb.htm
Jan's Abba Forever site is a winner. Takes it all, then.

Aerosmith http://www.hooked.net/users/noelh/aero.html
Nicole's Aerosmith Tribute Page is exceptionally busy, with

interviews, news articles (90 at the last count), quizzes, quotes, poems, parodies, a bootleg file, and even the substitute lyrics Steve Tyler uses live when, er, memory fails. All the best Aerosmith sites are reviewed on the grounds of content and originality – among many, many other things – in The Aeropit at http://www.geocities.com/SunsetStrip/palms/1519/aerosmith.html.

Aphex Twin   http://www.joyrex.com

The Aphex Twin Information Database is coloured a cool metallic blue and written in the funkiest typeface. Updated near-daily, it's arranged in sections with cold techno-headings such as 'Vizualisation' (for videos), 'Navigation' and 'Education', and is pleasantly arrogant and obsessive. There are neat poster offers, and fan art is on display, as well as those horrible pictures of the bearded Twin (or Richard D James as they respectfully title him on most fan sites) with his head transposed on to the body of a busty model. Ugh.

The B-52s   http://www.avatardesign.net/redplanet

Red Planet has brilliant, beautiful B-movie sci-fi graphics, with biogs, galleries and RealAudio downloads on offer. There are also fabulous and absolutely appropriate dancing cartoons of the band. When searching for other B-52 info, be careful to avoid http://www.af.mil/news/factsheets/B_52_stratofortress.html. This concerns the long-range heavy bomber and is not in the least bit funky or amusing. Unless you're into Sepultura or GWAR.

Backstreet Boys   http://www.geocities.com/
SunsetStrip/Palms/7002

Slow, but with some interesting bits. Visit the live chat room to share your opinions with other Backstreet Boys fans, plus links to the French and Canadian sites.

Beatles   http://www.geocities.com/~beatleboy1

Here the Ultimate Beatles Experience gives the history of the band
in their own words, over 200 rare and classic photos, Beatles email
greeting cards, interviews and animations. A must for all fans of
the definitive pop group.

Billie   http://www.mbuzz.co.uk/billie

As good as the official Virgin site and featuring a more
adventurous selection of pix and facts.

Black   http://www.ultranet.com/~geezer/
Sabbath   black_sabbath_game.html

This is listed as 6 Degrees of Ozzy Osbourne and is a metal version
of the legendary quiz featuring Kevin Bacon. It's not actually a
game in itself: its host Bill M simply provides answers to hundreds
of questions with which you can then torment your wannabe
cloven-hoofed mates. Can you connect the Sabs to Tony Bennett in
only six moves? Or the Beastie Boys? The Beatles? The Bee Gees?
Go on, we dare you.

Mary J. Blige   http://www.nyrock.com/blige.htm

'MJB – I wanna be your dog'. Not a bad woman-to-woman rant
here, with some fantastic old shots of the 90s diva. Amazingly, La
Blige's official site, at http://www.mjblige.com, is splendiferous
also. Music while we load, then the hi-tech sexiness takes over.

Blur   http://www.geocities.com/SoHo/Studios

The lengths some fans go to. Cuh! This Blur Cartoons site is
actually touching, sweet and occasionally very funny. These
cartoons and comic strips are good fun for fans and non-fans alike.
There's another good one, called Blur Talk, at http://www.
blurtalk.com. This one takes much of its info from the Blur FC site,
but making it available to everyone. Really good-looking and
professional, it is updated daily.

David Bowie   http://www.bowiewonderland.com

Bowie Wonderland is more conventional than BowieNet, but is in some ways a better bet for fans, containing anything and everything Bowie-related, including a healthy dose of humour, such as Anoraks Corner. Also check out 5 Years.Com at http://www.5years.com. This one obsessively documents the making and aftermath of the Definitive Rock 'n' Roll Concept Album. Nineteenseventytastic.

Tim   http://pantheon.cis.yale.edu/
Buckley   ~bodoin/tbarchives.html

Beautifully presented, the Tim Buckley Archives are simple, direct, loving and mature – just as you'd expect from sophisticated star sailors. Each album's lyrics and production information are covered, and news files acquaint you with the great man's sorry end and posthumous popularity. Apparently, he snorted heroin thinking it to be cocaine. A must for archivists and all sensitive souls.

The Cardigans   http://www.geocities.com/TelevisionCity/5099

Fairly dull-looking but notably anal, this base for 'CardiFans' allows you to drool over pictures of many a signed CD sleeve, and is overjoyed to link you to the band's Russian homepage. With a name like Sullen Sweaters, it has to be worth it – no?

Catatonia   http://easyweb.easynet.co.uk/
   ~durandal/catatonia/index.htm

One of the best Catatonia fan sites on the web – clearly laid out, lots of pictures and good writing.

Nick Cave   http://www.bad-seed.org

Dedicated to the man and his Seeds, this is a backcombed, skinny-trousered triumph. The Cave Inn at http://www.web4. integraonline. com/~cave/front.html is the largest Cave resource and very fine it is too. And for those keen on Nick the Stripper's literary efforts, look no further than King Ink at http://www. kingink.org. Did you know that 'Release the Bats' wasn't actually about bats? Gah, who'd be a goth?

The Clash   http://members.aol.com/clashcshow
In a world currently without a barnstorming Clash site, this is probably the best. Good news section on all ex-members' activities, re-release activity in the US and UK, plus rocking graphics. You might also care to catch up with Josef Strummereros at http://members.tripod.com/joe_strummer, which is a bang-up-to-date site with great pictures and good writing.

Chemical Brothers   http://uuuu.org/chemical
Chemical Schmemical contains a biography, a discography, pictures and links – it looks good and is better then the official site. Try Dustweb at http://www.unet.net/monaco/andrew/chemical too. This one's great fun. It even has a 'Lyrics' section. Hmm.

The Doors   http://www.geocities.com/
SunsetStrip/5281/concert.gif
The web is crammed with sites dedicated to the Lizard King. This one stands out. Jim would've loved it, if he hadn't been hounded to an early grave by The Man, man. Or so Olly Stone told us.

5ive   http://www.duplidata.co.uk/gemma/index.htm
5ive Central is considerably easier to access than the impregnable BMG Backstage. There are several links to other pages plus all the latest news and gossip about one of the best boy bands around.

Fleetwood Mac   http://www.cyberpenguin.net/penguin
The Penguin, as it's known, is the very best online resource for the Mac (that's Fleetwood Mac, not your computer) and includes all the latest news about and movements of all the members,

ex-members and affiliates. Of course, most of the interesting stuff concerns Stevie Nicks, but then that always was the case, wasn't it?

Marvin Gaye   http://www.sedgesoftware.com/marvin

By 'modest' Mark Sedgewick who offers his 'little tribute to the Main Man'. This fan page is so corking it's received over 2 million visits since it began. With RealAudio streams as well as great pictures, you needn't bother relying on the grapevine any more.

The Grateful Dead   http://www.dc.net/stanley

Shakedown Street – The GD Dictionary: this includes a full band history, downloads, Real Audio streams and pictures. It's a great Dead site. Not as much fun but still a must for fans – mainly due to the chat rooms – is Dead Net, at http://www.dead.net.

Geri Halliwell   http://www.trixiefirecracker.co.uk

A really impressive unofficial Geri website with all the usual, plus a 'Geri Of The Day' pic and loads of fun and games. Witty, irreverent and packed, just like Geri herself. If she had a gun, like.

Elton John   http://ej.kylz.com

The Illustrated Elton Discography and brilliantly constructed site for the John man. The only thing it lacks is a news section.

Tom Jones   http://www.geocities.com/
TheTropics/Island/6666/music.html

A lovingly crafted site from people who may possibly be a little obsessed. Imagine Deep Impact with panties instead of sea water.

Led Zeppelin   http://www.led-zeppelin.com

Award-winning Electric Magic unofficial site with highlights of the Zeps' history considered by article and thumbnail. You can stream rare video, check out Jimmy Page's fluctuating weight through three decades, or simply access the frequently updated news.

John Lennon   http://www.bagism.com
Run by one Sam Choukri, Bagism is the definitive Lennon site
packed with absolutely everything you could possibly want to
know or see, plus a healthy dose of submissions from fans.

Manic Street Preachers   http://www.manics.cjb.net
A good site with a great name – Archives of Pain. Excellent pictures
and a proper handle on the spirit and passion behind the band that
the official site lacks. More nude pictures of Sean though, please.
Er, one maybe? Sorry, only joking.

Bob Marley   http://members.aol.com/travisnd/page/inter.html
Known as the Bob Marley Unofficial Site, this one looks spectacular
with lots of up-to-date content. Really professional. Every picture
scan in the large library is transparency quality and there are some
great quotes and links.

Paul McCartney   http://rgo.simplenet.com/macca
Plugged: The Unofficial McCartney Homepage is, as it says, an
unofficial, but pretty definitive site for Macca fans. All the latest
news, bootlegs, a complete discography and high-quality scans,
plus loads of Beatles links. Ahoy! Thumbs aloft!

George   http://www.geocities.com/
Michael   SunsetStrip/Palms/9988/picson.jpg
Unsocial Mix is very good for those wanting the pictures and the
music, but hasn't been updated for ages because the host is
'moving to a new town'. Cuh, fan sites! Wake us up before you
go-go.

The Monkees   http://www.themonkees.com/webpages.html
Great photo-scans, TV-show listings, music and news. A brilliant
site.

Nirvana   http://www.digitalnirvana.net

Enormous, completist, and good-looking site with much about the Foo Fighters as well. You might also be interested in Grungers' Corner at http://www.grungers-corner.com. Great links to many other Cobain-related stuff on the web.

Gary Numan   http://www.garynumanfan.nu

When you read a header like 'A home on the web for fans of the greatest musician in all of explored space', and then you realise they're talking about Gary Numan – Gazza, for Gawd's sake – you know you're in for a treat. Especially on the message boards. If this is not enough, check out the Gazman's own immense site at http://www.numan.co.uk, which contains The Alien Magazine. And if that's not enough, you are a Numanoid and should seek professional help immediately. There's a man at the window smoking a cigarette, indeed.

Oasis   http://www.the oasis.force9.co.uk

The Oasis.co.uk. Updated daily with news from all sources, and links to a hundred other top sites for the band, this is much better than the official site.

Ocean Colour Scene   http://www.redhorn.demon.co.uk

OCS Central is one of the best sites in an overcrowded genre, full of links for the Brummie mod rockers.

Iggy Pop   http://www.contrib.andrew.cmu.edu/~jacquez/iggy

This looks like an official site due to the good-looking and informed feel it has. With masses of photos and up-to-date news, it's better than The Ig's Virgin site.

Pulp   http://www.jeigh.com/pulp/

Lovingly put together, all this site needs now is for the band to do something new.

Elvis Presley   **http://www.elvispresleyonline.com**
A well-written fan site for the man responsible for worldwide irresponsibility, it bristles with stacks of high-quality picture scans from GI to Fatboy and is updated daily. Saw him yesterday, as it happens. He's lost a lot of weight.

Queen   **http://www.brunssum.net/wbuczko/index2.html**
Since 1997 the Queen Picture Hall has been the site for all Fandango-fans, boasting a massive picture library, collector's-item price lists, hundreds of links and even some MP3s. There's also an excellent effort from the Queen Fan Club, Queen World, which is easy to use and well informed. Find it at **http://www.queenworld.com**.

Smokey Robinson   **http://www3.edgenet.net/smokey_miracles**
This is the fan club homepage and is brilliant for all the latest and greatest on Smokey Robinson and his Miracles. There's also a definitive section of links to other Motown artists.

Sex   **http://www.rockmine.music.co.uk/**
Pistols   **Pistols/Jordan.JPG**
A brilliant archive of original Pistols artefacts like the original 1977 press release, rare photographs of the band and a transcription of the swearing-on-live-TV debacle with Bill Grundy – that rotter. There's a more music-orientated Pistols site, including guitar tabs for all the tunes, at **http://www.users.wineasy.se/ludde/pics.htm**

The Smiths/Morrissey   **http://shoplifters.morrissey-solo.com**
Shoplifters Union proclaims itself to be Your Guide to Morrissey and the Smiths on the Internet and it more than fulfils that promise. Definitive.

Britney Spears   **http://4britneyspears.homepage.com**
The 4Britney-Colouring Book is a charming site where you may print off pictures of the young star to colour in at your leisure.

Rod Stewart   http://members.aol.com/hannuschka/lyrics
This, called Lyrics, is a must for fans of the evergreen singer – lyrics to every song he has ever sung, including his guest appearances.

Travis   http://members.tripod.com/~yeoyl/title.jpg
Pasted together with blood, sweat and Prittstick, The Men Who is a rough and almost ready site, dedicated to the little Scottish fellows who unexpectedly ran off with 1999.

Tina   http://www.btinternet.com/
Turner   ~craigbardsley/main.html
Bang up to date and easy to use, Nothing But Tina is a must for fans.

Shania   http://www.geocities.com/
Twain   SunsetStrip/Venue/8103/mainlogo.jpg
Forever Shania. A complete guide to the genre-smashing Country Queen who'd like us all to refer to her as Eilleen now that she's famous, please, if you don't mind.

U2   http://www.atu2.com
A reliable and informative fan website, stuffed with up-to-date news and pictures – and it's easily navigable. A jewel in the cow pat of self-indulgent U2 fan websites.

Paul Weller/   http://www.skynet.co.uk/
The Jam   ~kefansu/the_jam/frames.html
One man's obsession with winkle-pickers shared with the world.

Westlife   http://come.to/westlife
The Worldwide Westlife Website is really well put together, packed with all the 'Life info you want and need. Blimey, Nicky's going out with the Irish Prime Minister Bertie Aherne's daughter! And we all thought he …

7//MP3: WHAT IT IS AND HOW IT WORKS

Nineteen ninety-nine was the year 'MP3' overtook 'sex' as the most oft-sought keyword on the Internet. The reason is clear. With its massive underground and independent popularity, the MP3 format has threatened to tear control of music distribution from the hands of record companies and, paying no heed to the rights of either the companies or the recording artists themselves, it has made it possible for music to be taken, free of charge, by anyone with a sound-enabled PC and the right (easily available) software.

Beyond punk, or acid house, or even rock 'n' roll itself, MP3 is reckoned to be absolutely revolutionary.

As an idea, it's pretty simple. MP3 is the common name given to MPEG Audio Layer 3 files, Layer 3 being one of three coding schemes allowing for the compression of audio signals (there are also Layers 1 and 2). What it does is shrink a CD's original sound data by a factor of about 12, taking the bit rate (basically the number of zeroes and ones used to 'describe' sound in a digital form) of 1,411.2 kilobits per one second of stereo music down to 112.128kbps. There's little or no reduction in sound quality, as MP3 works by cutting out all superfluous information – that is all the unimportant bits of a sound signal that our ears don't pick up anyway. This process is popularly known as 'ripping'. If you really wish to know all the techie details about perceptual audio coding, psychoacoustic compression and how a filter bank increases the frequency resolution to 18 times that of Layer 2, look up MP3 at About.com or the mighty Webopedia (www.webopedia.com).

Invented in 1991 by researchers at the German Fraunhofer Institute, the MPEG file-compression format was initially developed for broadcast purposes – no surprise then that the MPEG should stand for the Motion Picture Experts Group. But it eventually made it on to the Internet where, because it crushes files so effectively, making them easier to transfer, it was recognised as the very best method of sending music back and forth.

Why record companies are worried

The format has been controversial from the start, putting the wind up record companies for two main reasons: (a) there is no loss of sound quality when copying digitally and (b) a single MP3 file on the Net is available to literally millions of consumers. Bootlegging was never too much of a problem before because of cassette hiss and deterioration, and the fact that, well, how many people make tapes up for their friends? Only now has equipment for 'burning' (copying) CDs become widely available and reasonably priced – and most people still can't be bothered.

MP3, though, might well make the easy and cheap production of high-quality copies a reality. At the moment, for most people, the process is slow, tracks taking minutes to download. A lot of MP3 downloading is done surreptitiously in the workplace where people can get access to far more powerful systems than the ones they have at home. But the ever more widespread cable modem, which can connect your computer to the Internet via a TV company's cable, will increase the speed at which you receive data by between 40 and 200 times. And then there are DSL (Digital Subscriber Lines) and ADSL (Asymmetric Digital Subscriber Lines), which work over standard telephone cables. These are already generally available in some countries, and will allow MP3 files to be downloaded in seconds. That future is almost upon us, and already is upon many.

All you require to download MP3 files right now is an application to decode the format, and there are dozens available for you to download free of charge. In late 1999, WinAmp, who make the most popular shareware MP3 player and now form part of the AOL empire, reckoned that over 5 million people had already downloaded their program, and thus turned their computers into MP3 music libraries. For info on how to upload MP3s – that is, put your own music on a website so that others can download it – see Chapter 9.

Enter the portable player
For anyone who for some reason doesn't want their computer to act as a home listening system, or likes to rock when they're out and about, there is a rapidly increasing number of compact, portable, Walkman-like players available, which store MP3 files in solid-state memory and can often be plugged into your home stereo or the system in your car. Though some can be a tad unwieldy and some take memory from a problematic flash card, they are improving by leaps and bounds. All manner of services are provided by the new generation of players. The Lyra, for instance, allows you to store up to six hours of music. Many allow you to make text memos and voice recordings, and even operate as phone books, a bit like personal organisers. Some are so brilliantly pernickety, they let you save and repeat tiny bits of tracks, maybe your favourite guitar freak-out, or John Bonham's drum solo in Led Zeppelin's 'Moby Dick' (though that hardly constitutes a 'tiny bit').

You needn't just stick to music, either. Audible.com let you download magazines, newspapers and books on to your MP3 player, and some players have bookmarks so you can keep your place in Ike Turner's lurid memoirs, or the latest in-depth analysis of

Bob Dylan's rebellious use of punctuation on 'Highway 61 Revisited'. You'll find the best of everything listed below.

What you can expect
So easy is the MP3 process that MP3 sites have proliferated like flies, and many have expanded exponentially. MP3.com, for instance, has hundreds of thousands of tracks available for download. Most e-retailers have lists of MP3 files compiled for your listening pleasure. Some record companies and many magazines are in on the act, and even official band sites provide them. There are presently literally millions of songs out there, waiting just for you, many of them downloadable for nothing.

Unfortunately, most of them are terrible, uploaded by unsigned bands keen to gain an audience via this new technology, and so circumvent record companies and the usual business channels (and, naturally, rake in a higher percentage of any profits accrued). Some MP3 sites operate some form of quality-control system, making available only tracks the controllers believe to be of a sufficiently high standard. Others, though, charge bands for their services, or cannot attract enough bands to their site, and these will present you with just about anything. If you ever thought daytime radio was trite, trashy and peopled by incompetents, well, the world of MP3 will shake you to the core. Anyone can get up there – so they do. And, as Sid Vicious so accurately spat all those years ago, 99 per cent is shit.

There is that other 1 per cent, though, and they can be spectacularly impressive. Because most MP3s are from bands who are poor and unsigned, the sound quality can be relatively dire even before compression takes place. They just don't have the money for studios, producers, mixers, or even adequate equipment. Consequently, you're unlikely to stumble across acts exhibiting the pyrotechnic production techniques of, say, Queen or Peter Gabriel. But, if you're looking for something a little simpler, you may be served well. The Internet is legendarily full of surprises.

Dance, in many of its forms, takes to MP3 like a proverbial duck. Raging techno can work this way, as can dreamy, chilled-out ambient. Consequently, MP3 sites specialising in dance, for instance Crunch, can offer some true marvels for the aficionado. Any genre that can be effectively recorded in the bedroom or on the cheap – trashy rock, acoustic versions, trip-hop or dub – is worth checking out on the better unsigned band sites.

Pay as you play
MP3 sites can vary wildly in style, content and purpose. Some, like Scour (http://scout.net/) or 2Look4 (http://www.2look4.com/), are search engines that will seek out MP3 files of any band whose name you key in. Others, such as Emusic (http://www.emusic.com), have massive lists of files from established artists, available on a pay-to-download basis, usually costing a basic 99 cents a track. You'll no doubt end up buying CDs too. The best MP3 sites will allow you to listen to a band's tracks, and download some of them, sometimes for nothing, more often for a nominal sum.

But to get everything available by that band you'll have to cough up for a standard CD, which the MP3 site will 'burn' and post to you on request. As most of the bands are unheard of and keen for you to possess their material and spread the word round to all your friends, prices are usually very reasonable – $6 an album is not untypical. Mind you, as we saw earlier, it's likely that very little has been spent on production, and you'll certainly not be receiving a flashy CD with a 3-D cover and a booklet packed with glossy photos by Annie Liebowitz or Anton Corbijn.

As far as organisation goes, expect artists to be listed by genre, and expect the lists to be long. Naturally, as with any kind of enforced categorisation, acts will end up in the wrong list, and you may find yourself listening to tracks that annoy you beyond all reason. But there are usually reviews there to guide you, and sometimes even well-informed features, so bear with it. The bigger MP3 sites, like the mighty and now-notorious MP3.com, will generally provide you with excellent information about the acts they include. Bands receive at least a page's worth of space, allowing for pictures and biographical info. The sites' controllers will, for the most part, review the music themselves, their opinions being to the point, if a little grey, though sometimes bands are invited to review each other. This normally results is a revolting fiesta of craven back-scratching, but can sometimes turn hilariously nasty. In the world of unsigned bands, there are an awful lot of needy, competitive and bitter people – and here they all are, for your entertainment.

If you look around, you'll find a fair number of major acts offering songs for free. The theory behind such apparent altruism is this. Acts traditionally release singles to promote forthcoming or current LPs (LPs being where the big profits lie), yet printing up, distributing and promoting singles can be a terribly expensive business – particularly if no albums are sold. Making a track available on MP3 involves none of these costs, and still creates a buzz. Some big bands, TLC and Sebadoh for example, have even begun to give away tracks on sites usually dedicated to unsigned acts, thereby dominating the sites' charts and securing what is, to all intents, a constant and impressive advert for themselves.

Some sites allow only one downloadable track per band, others permit an entire album. Punters can download tracks (usually for a buck apiece), or order CDs, which the controllers will 'burn' and post to your home – the profits to be split with the bands, often at a generous 50/50 percentage cut. Be prepared for a fair number of adverts cluttering the screen. MP3 sites who offer their services free to bands need to make money somehow, and this is one way they do it. You'll sometimes even hear audio ads dropped in before the tracks you've clicked on, like at the cinema but more irritating.

A cyber club for all?

MP3 sites generally pride themselves on offering more than just music. Because technology has not quite advanced far enough for all of us to enjoy the super-rapid transfer of data, the world of MP3 remains relatively small and still maintains an indie attitude that's very community-friendly. For many, the sites, with their own charts and statistics (totally independent of The Man, dude) and their own chat rooms and message boards, are places to get together with like-minded individuals. Land-based magazines have sporadically tried to do this but always eventually failed, being unable to deliver the direct communication between music lovers now provided by the Internet.

The result is that MP3 sites can act as serious forums for musical debate, or simply as little indie clubs, where you can make friends and influence people. Sites will usually prominently display a figure revealing the weight of traffic passing through. If their Number One featured track has been downloaded only 200 times and appears to be about bats, congratulations! You're in goth heaven. But, if your wardrobe is not characterised by the absence of colour, don't be too fast to move on – indie message boards, with their vitriolic 'flame wars', wherein profoundly subjective arguments reach unheard-of levels of intensity, can be hugely amusing for the outsider (and not just those from the Albert Camus school of Outsidership).

//ADDRESS BOOK

Search Engines

Back in Chapter 3, we listed the search engines best equipped to track down whatever you were after – guitars, posters, albums, sheet music, you name it. Here we're giving you the lowdown on those engines that'll zip you straight to any MP3 file you could possibly imagine. These are the MP3 specialists ...

2LOOK4.com   http://www.2look4.com

Cleverly, this search engine has got over the problem of broken-down links by removing them from its index automatically after five tries, which thus reduces frustration. Good tips for beginners too.

Audiofind   http://www.audiofind.com

This slick search engine kicks off by giving a list of the most popular searches and then allows us to do the typing thing and go our own way. It has a great feel and is very fast.

Dimension Music   http://www.dimensionmusic.com

A stylish MP3 search engine with a great news section full of tales of dastardly deeds in the music business. Simply punch in your selected genre or artist and this little beauty will do its best to find you something. Very recommended.

Listen.com   http://www.listen.com

Describes itself as 'Your guide to MP3 and more'. It's a search engine, listing websites that carry MP3, Liquid and other audio formats, and includes a Big Shots section with lists of established names like REM, Cheap Trick and the Chemical Brothers.

Lycos   http://mp3.lycos.com

Claiming to have over a million MP3 files to download, this is a relatively new search engine. The bands are largely unsigned unheard-ofs, but to comply with the Secure Digital Music Initiative (SDMI) this is hardly surprising. Unfortunately, the directory appears to have been compiled by someone unfamiliar with traditional pop music genre categorisation or, indeed, logic.

MP3Board.com   http:www.mp3board.com

Deceptively simple-looking search field trawls for MP3s you type in. We tried Led Zeppelin and a song by Christina Aguilera: both queries came back with reams of stuff.

MP3 Media   http://broadcast.go.com/mp3

A good place to start, this is part of the Go Network and offers an MP3 Express search engine to race through the web and find downloadables of your choice. Other than that, there is a list of name-artist downloads gleaned from other sites, most of which are free. Cheers!

Scour   http://www.scour.net

Not just looking out for MP3s but also webcasts, video and webradio, Scour is the best place to search for the streaming format, i.e. music or images in streamed (rather than downloadable) form. Don't panic: it does downloads too. Recommended.

Sites For Quality New Artists

Amazon.com   http://www.amazon.com

You may be bored of reading about Amazon by now, but, in addition to everything else, they do have music downloads to buy as well.

Crunch   http://www.crunch.co.uk

UK-based and geared more towards dance music; links with underground indie labels such as Pussyfoot, Dishy and Nuphonic add kudos, as does an alternative page with occasional hook-ups with larger labels. Includes extensive back cats, rarities, exclusive DJ mixes and live performances from clubs and venues across the planet. Tracks tend not to be free, but are usually no more than 99 pence each.

CDNow   **http://www.cdnow.com**

One of the best places for new bands with free downloads as well as some established artists, with MP3s to flog. There's quite a good basic guide to the whole MP3 shebang, too.

Cductive   **http://digital.cductive.com**

Now part of Emusic, this has a brilliant selection of dance-orientated/alternative artists and labels. Some tracks are free, but most of the well-known stuff is 99 cents a track. You can also create you own compilation CD for the same price. From Elliott Smith to Coldcut!

Emusic   **http://www.emusic.com**

Massive US organisation that focuses more on pay-to-download tracks (mainly 99 cents) from established artists, plus some free tracks from big guns such as Bush, Joe Strummer and Phish. Predominantly rock-orientated but does feature some Dance and Electronica.

Mad As A Fish   **http://www.madasafish.com**

Not exclusively music-orientated, MAAF is a store, linked to a search engine, which offers movies and games too. There are several free MP3s available weekly and the quality of the artists is generally pretty fine.

Music Grab   **http://www.musicgrab.com**

Great that an MP3 site – usually reluctant to acknowledge the existence of any competition – can offer a useful page of links. With

Music Grab we can search the web for name artists and find whether there is anything legal out there. Of course, typing in 'the Beatles' gets you Beatle-tribute bands, and the promising Pink Floyd links come to nothing, but this is a worthwhile place, nonetheless.

MP3.Com   http://www.mp3.com

For a long time the scourge of record companies, the mother of all MP3 sites has now gone legitimate, with co-operation from its former enemies. The scope is vast and genre-rich, stretching from Californian straight-edge to Celtic folk to comedy. There is lots of free music, advice for beginners, software downloads, as well as a 'Women On MP3' section devoted to female artists.

MP3 World   http://www.www.worldkey.com/mp3world/

A good archive of downloads some of which are free, all of which are legal. The genre listing could be a little bit clearer.

Peoplesound.com   http://www.peoplesound.com

The artists are of a good standard here, which is largely down to the A&R element, often missing on MP3 sites. Despite the quality, the question remains: do we really want to find music that 'sounds like' something we already know? A good tip is to rename your chosen files, once they've been downloaded – they are difficult to access if left as they are, because they are in unmemorable telephone-number code, making it a nightmare to distinguish between tracks.

Vitaminic   http://www.vitaminic.co.uk

Europe's so-called largest MP3 site features a Top Ten download on the homepage, which is packed with major names. There are also hundreds of unknowns that we can experiment with via audio stream, before we decide to buy or not.

Yawho.com   **http://www.yawho.com**

Not to be confused with the similar-sounding ubiquitous portal, this is a pretty basic library of interesting artists offering their files for free download. It has a good software section, too.

Newer Sites

MP3 is a revolutionary innovation, and new MP3 sites are springing up on an hourly basis. The following, though still fairly inconsequential at the time of writing, seem set for massive expansion and, possibly, world domination.

Aggressive Music   **http://www.aggressivemusic.com**

This is designed for musicians; guitar tablature accompanies each track, plus lyrics and other muso-information such as equipment and recording techniques used. The selection is small at the moment but it is surely an idea that will appeal across the board.

Eat Sleep Music   **http://www.eatsleepmusic.com/tunes/mp3**

Growing out of a karaoke site, this is actually a good place to find free downloads from up-and-coming bands. Choose from a wide range of genres. They also feature some established artists.

Kermit   **http://www.oth.net**

Unbelievably fast and simple: punch anything into the simple search field and, before your finger has left the keyboard, there is a list of MP3 files in front of you. Displays only file names, not song titles, but it is a living argument to cut back on flashy graphics in favour of speeding up searching.

MP3now.com   **http://www.mp3now.com**

Part of the Change Music Network (which has just merged with CMJ – the USA's most respected alternative-music information network), this offers all you would expect from a company who promise to introduce consumers to the best new music first. There is additional magazine-style news as well as good biographies of all the artists featured.

MP3.dk http://www.mp3.dk
Everything you need to know about MP3 and the latest developments on the web, so you don't have to appear stupid when talking to your clued-up mates.

MP3 2000 http://www.mp3-2000.com
Not live at the time of writing, but there is much anticipation. Promises daily updated news, music reviews and more than usual interactivity.

MP3 Players

Jazpiper http://www.jazpiper.nl
Well-rounded sound, a rapid transfer rate, a mighty sunken button for easy access, plus a host of unusual extras, including the ability to endlessly replay your favourite guitar solos, drum rolls or lyrical fancies. Accidental erasing might be a problem.

Lyra http://www.lyrazone.com
Relatively big and heavy and indisputably ugly, the Lyra is otherwise brilliant, with audible track scanning, a five-band EQ and a backlit display showing artist, album and track info. Lyra will also support the IBM Microdrive, holding 340Mb (six whole hours!) of sound.

MPlayer3 http://www.mplayer3.com
Most players have preset modes for rock, jazz and classical but this, Pontis's top-grade European model, has adjustable bass and treble, allowing for excellent tone. It's also compatible with Mac and Linux systems. Unfortunately, it's fairly heavy, downloading is slow and, with no onboard memory, it limits users to a frighteningly exposed flash card.

MPMan F20   http://www.mpman.com

Saehan's MPMan was released in competition to the Rio but lacked the promotional muscle to win out. This second-generation model stores all manner of files (.txt, .gif, .doc etc.), and a massively improved and expanded product line is expected soon.

Nomad   http://www.nomadworld.com

Tough and cool-looking with a magnesium sheen, this comes with a voice recorder, a helpfully prominent LCD display and a belt clip (a rare joy). The docking station connecting it to your computer takes up desktop space but does recharge the player and set its time display.

Ravemp   http://www.ravemp.com

Sensory Science's Ravemp – with its slim, hourglass figure, superb Sennheiser earbuds, sizeable onboard memory and an auto-resume, which starts the music wherever it stopped – also features non-music additions such as text memos, voice recording and a phone book.

Rio PMP500   http://www.rioport.com

The second-generation Rio comes in a cute, i-Mac-style translucent purple or teal casing, and features plenty of additions, most notably a cassette adapter for use with your car stereo. Also allows you to store mixes and place bookmarks in MP3 audio books, and is compatible with Audible.com's hugely useful collection of magazines, newspapers and books.

Yepp   http://www.yepp.co.kr

Samsung's Yepp Series E has large buttons and a three-line display, plus voice recording, a phone book and a neat blue or silver shell. Best of all, there's a 3-D-audio feature giving extra-spacey sound.

8//MUSIC, MUSIC, MUSIC

You'd now be hard-pressed to find a musical artist of any repute who doesn't run, or oversee the running of, their own site. Competition and the consequent importance of self-promotion, as well as increased awareness of the artistic liberty permitted by the Internet, mean that many of these sites are now unarguably excellent, offering all manner of information and musical material hitherto unavailable. Acts' efforts to keep their sites funky, colourful and wild will mean you'll probably need both Flash and a decent listening system to fully appreciate them but, as with Madonna's Maverick site, these are often available for download at the band site itself.

Naturally, bands do like to sell their own material. Most sites, even the less corporate ones, will prod you towards parting with your money every step of the way. Though Internet sales are presently fairly low – October 1999 saw Billboard's Top Internet Album Sales chart topped by the far-from-famous bar band Roger Clyne & the Peacemakers, who'd shifted only around 1,200 copies of their LP – this is bound to change as consumer spending habits alter.

Thanks, Jessica and Macy

One impressive modern site is that of the Christian pop starlet Jessica Simpson (http://www.jessicasimpson.com). This provides you with chart info, screensavers and the chance to chat live with other Jessica fans. You can buy her CDs, merchandise and 'apparel', vote for your favourite Simpson song, watch her videos in QuickTime or RealVideo, enjoy an interview complete with audio and video clips, and even download an 18-minute MP3 file of young Jessica chatting about touring, dating and life in general. You can join the official fan club, send your friends a Jessica postcard complete with audio, as well as keep up with Jessica's cute and tasteful diary. There's also the occasional special, such as the live Valentine's Day chat with Jessica and her beau, Nick Lachey of the pop sensations 98 Degrees.

Other sites possess further added extras. Macy Gray's, for example (http://www.macygray.com), features a video biography in RealVideo, various attachments to make your emails more attractive, an opportunity to help choose her next single and some excellently tended message boards that have the decency to tell you when they've been added to. Her short-story competition was a genuinely innovative move that threw down the artistic gauntlet before all other acts, forcing them to think a little harder about exactly how interactive and entertaining their sites really were. Inspirational stuff.

Some acts link their sites to those of others, in an effort to guide their fans towards music they might also enjoy. They might also link to the sites of their own musical influences in order to help explain the origins of their own music. Some go further, linking to sites they hope fans will find amusing, outrageous or informative. Marilyn Manson, for instance, devotes his opening page (http://www.marilynmanson.net) to links taking you to the sites of conspiracy theorists, death-obsessed fantasists and money-hungry Baptist fundamentalists worldwide. He also links to the best fan sites dedicated to him – some even more lewd and confrontational than his own – and includes other links, enabling fans to install RealPlayer or MS Windows Media Player, so as to fully appreciate Manson's wicked oeuvre.

Other acts take a more positivist line. The Levellers – one of the first bands to truly embrace this new technology – provide information on, and link to, many political activists. Their site at **www. levellers.co.uk** is consequently one of the most powerful, challenging and fascinating in the musical arena.

What an act might do with their site has few limits. Some pay little attention, failing to update news or picture files, allowing their sites to stagnate. Most, though, use the chance to give their fans something extra – printed lyrics, new tracks, unseen photos, candid biographical info, quizzes, cartoons, animations and funny pages. You'll often find competitions too, sometimes with very worthwhile prizes. Usually you'll just be winning CDs, T-shirts and assorted merchandise, but Keith Richards' guitar was once on offer.

Rock star – or Internet hub?

Then there are the big ones. When an act is rich and interested, they can genuinely test the boundaries of interaction. Back in 1998, Dave Stewart of Eurythmics played a show at his Church Studio that was broadcast live on to screens in clubs across Europe. That evening, he also wrote a song live on Internet, accepting suggestions from his fans and thus co-writing with them. The track was recorded, mixed and made available for download within a few hours – the fastest ever.

And there's David Bowie, whose site **www.david.bowie.com** often claimed to be the best of all. Aside from state-of-the-art graphics, he also offers a gallery of his own artwork, and another one with exhibits from the notorious Sensation exhibition of young British artists that so offended New York's Mayor Giuliani. Bowie also allows you to download a Beatnik Player 2.0, the first ever music technology to offer interactive MP3 on the web. Then, setting up your own combination of drums, bass, guitar and backing vocals, you can move around Bowie's lead vocals to create your own mix of his song 'Fame'. Originally, this was a competition, the winner being flown to New York to record with Bowie face to face. Incredible what you find when you look.

And it's fun
But beyond the official sites and the fan sites there's so much more out there. Where most people believed and still believe the world of land-based publishing to be a closed shop – no platform for the uninteresting, uneducated likes of us! – the Internet has offered a new freedom. Not having to perform in front of a live audience, being able to say anything at all without any fear of embarrassment, you're sheltered by the Net, which protects you, and encourages you to follow your interests and obsessions to the end. It allows you to dare.

Where else would we ever have been able to find something a strange and enjoyable as Warp A Spice Girl (**http://members.tripod.com/~grantmcl/warpspicegirls.html**), where we get to experiment with (virtually) pulling around the faces of four of the most famous women in the world? Where else could we watch Geri Halliwell explode, or see Posh in claymation?

And it's not just about the ubiquitous wannabes. Below you'll find pointers to the best of jazz, reggae and soul, world music and punk, plus loving journeys through each of the last five decades. You'll find the very best sites devoted to the very biggest artists, and some – such as I Hate Mariah and The Beatles Suck Homepage – that just aren't that respectful. They're all there, Belle & Sebastian, B*Witched, Beefheart, Beck and Billie.

There's the wildest fun to be found. Check out the Myths of the Music Biz, the Random Band Name Generator, the site dedicated to mullet hairdos, the notorious Rock School site, and another about the Rutles. And we haven't even mentioned the one about Mick Hucknall's genitalia. It's all you ever wanted, and quite a lot of things you didn't. Read on and revel in this newfound liberty. Enjoy ...

//ADDRESS BOOK

50s Music

Time to break out the Brylcreem, the winkle-pickers and that rather becoming purple crêpe jacket. Quifftastic!

Sun Records http://www.sunstudio.com
The birthplace of rock 'n' roll has produced a site that makes you want to get on a plane and go there. There's a fun tour of the studio plus a flea market stuffed with old 45s and rock 'n' roll memorabilia. Fifteen coaches long!

The Wanderer http://www.wanderers.com/wanderer
Claims to be the finest oldies site on the web; 50s and 60s songs are recreated by the Wanderer on his hilarious home keyboard.

Oldies http://www.oldiesmusic.com
Lovingly compiled, containing all the information you could ever want on the 50s and 60s.

Classic http://www.geocities.com/
Madhatter Broadway/9476/madhat.html
Links to the best live entertainers in the world – Sinatra, Bennett, Bassey and Bing with a bong. Not that Bing ever had a bong, you understand.

60s Music

All you wanted to know about the most innovative, exciting and off-its-face decade in the history of music. Started with the Beatles, ended at Altamont but kept on going in the mind of poor old Oliver Stone.

British Pop Culture   http://www.sixtiespop.com
A trawl from beatnik through to psychedelia, with much music content.

Mystic Fog   http://www.acs.ucalgary.ca/~fvigneau
Billed as the 'Psychedelic Music Page', this has some great links plus a wealth of blissed-out sound and hazy images. The webmaster, methinks, had way too much to dream last night.

A Psychedelic   http://www.lib.virginia.eduexhibits/
Sixties Music Page   sixties/rock.html
From the university of Virginia; some good scans of classic album sleeves plus biographical details.

The Sixties   http://www.slip.net/~scmetro/sixties.htm
Award-winning site on every aspect of the decade, but really surpassing itself on the music front.

70s Music

Disco, glam, prog and punk – the 70s was surely the silliest of decades. Consequently, the following sites should be everyone's first port of call. Come on, get up, stand up, strut your funky stuff!

A Biased History Of Glam Rock   http://www.doremi.co.uk/glam
Fab. Lots of useful sparkly platformed links too.

Disco Inferno	http://hem.passagen.se/
discoguy/artists/artists.html

Decent and reliable guide to disco heaven. A little drab, especially considering the notorious decadence of the gold medallion-wearing, platform-stomping, sex-obsessed subject matter. Aah, when the feelin's gone and you can't go on ...

Saturday Night Fever	http://room34.com/snf

Beautifully constructed homage to the movie and its music. Ha! Ha! Ha! Ha! Stayin' Aliiiiiii-iiive!!!

Seventies Dance Music Page	http://izan.simplenet.com/70.html

Great links for your favourite artists, from Sister Sledge to Gibson Brothers. Get on up! Now, get on down!

Super Seventies	http://www.geocities.com/
Rock Site	SunsetStrip/8678

Top 100s, a pop quiz, a photo gallery, year-by-year accounts, star reminiscences, tons of links and other nostalgia.

Vintage	http://www.geocities.com/SunsetStrip/
Classic Rock	Theater/5441/music.html

Links to the Stones, Neil Young, Bowie, Emerson Lake and Palmer, Deep Purple and many more. Blodwyn Pig album sleeves galore.

The Progressive Rock Website	http://www.progrock.net

Pretty fine, and with a suspicious overattention to detail, there is also 'Gibraltar' – a newsletter dedicated to obscure prog rock.

80s Music

The success of the Adam Sandler movie The Wedding Singer proved two things for sure - that the 80s really were as awful as we remember them to be, and that people can have a great time no matter what they're wearing or listening to. The following sites

whisk you back to fashion's darkest decade, when kilts, mullets and tight leather trousers were deemed the height of sartorial elegance. The horror ... the horror ...

Dance Music Of The Eighties http://www.andwedanced.com
Needs a few more years to complete the decade, but will suffice for now.

The 80's Server http://www.80s.com/Entertainment/music
From Cyndi Lauper to the Buggles. Yes, that's right – one truly great musical decade. This allows you to relive all those monumental moments when, just like Chandler from the US sitcom *Friends*, you looked as if five punk Mohican cuts had fallen on you from out of a tree. You never looked like that? Oh, well, why not play games while listening to the Thompson Twins instead?

In The 80s.Com http://www.inthe80s.com/bands
A massive index, stretching from Aha to Wide Boy Awake (remember them?), each name a reminder of the decade when everything went brilliantly for Thatcher, Reagan and the Masters of the Universe, and tragically badly for everyone else. There's a misheard-lyric section here which deserves extensive browsing. Remember Wang Chung? 'Take your baby by the ears, and play upon her doggie spheres'. Er, OK.

Moulin Noir http://www.moulin-noir.com/newromantic.html
An A-Z directory of the fashion disaster that was New Romance. 'Elegance, Energy, Melody', they say here. Surely, they can't mean A Flock of Seagulls.

Alternative/Indie

Channel Fly http://www.channelfly.com
A great UK indie music magazine with reviews, listings and even a

venue guide. A bit light on content at the moment but it feels as if they will get there.

CMJ http://www.cmj.com
Documenting, perhaps better than anyone, the progress of alternative-music culture in the US, this site is a magazine, a good links page and a good place to search for stuff. You can also find out about the annual conference organised by CMJ every year, which is the music industry's Cannes.

Epitonic http://www.epitonic.com
An alternative music store where every artist and label on the site has been hand-picked to help you guys stop wasting your bandwidth.

The Last Resort http://www.verdis.co.uk/TLR/resort.htm
Highly recommended UK indie-zine, which offers an expert guide to the scene, plus news, contacts and links, all constantly updated to never be behind the times.

The Local Scene http://www.thelocalscene.com
A great community of US indie bands, tips on how to find a bass player, and plenty of new music to listen to.

The Muse http://www.muse.ie
Very convincing Irish alternative music e-zine with good writing, interesting features and a feisty attitude. Looks good, too.

The Official Indie List http://www.bloofga.org/il/IL_FAQ.html
Available as a weekly updated newsletter, this site offers a clear explanation of what is going on in the world of US alternative music.

Pop Star Net http://www.popstar.net
An alternative pop page worth it alone for its fantastic 'International Popoverthrow' section.

Revolution   http://www.riot.co.uk

Independent UK alternative club-promotion marketing company and seminal Camden know-alls deliver a website of the highest order – all the forthcoming releases previewed, complete tour dates, the latest dance-floor charts plus links to the websites of every UK alternative artist, label and zine. So the revolution will be televised after all.

Rock Band.com   http://www.rockband.com

A US unsigned indie music site which is easy to navigate and contains some quite convincing bands.

Rocket Fuel Online   http://www.rocket-fuel.com

Big attitude and much whingeing about not-getting-paid-for-doing-it from the writers of this informed and slightly miserable alternative e-zine.

Shake it up   http://www3.sympatico.ca/cms.cas

Brilliant US power pop site covering vintage classics like the Beach Boys and modern stuff such as the High Llamas and the Posies.

Twomp Pop   http://www.twomp.com/pop

A hub page for great alternative Pop resources such as Shake It Up, Amplifier and Pure Pop.

The UK Indie   http://www.ee.surrey.ac.uk/
Band Index   Personal/S.Procter/UK-Indie/Links

Loads of useful band and label links, some of which, it must be said, don't work. Any self-respecting indie fan should bookmark this immediately. And the logo looks like a Kit Kat.

The Wonderwall   http://www.beat.co.uk/wonderwall.html

A bit like listening to a sixth-former shouting but, that aside, a site for sore ears. Links to all the key indie players, and some you forgot even existed.

XFM http://www.xfm.co.uk
Slow, content-light and dull. Oh dear. The only advantage of this site is the ability it gives you to listen to the station while you browse. Which is useful for those not living in London.

Ambient

Ambience For The Masses http://www.sleepbot.com/ambience
Search for the label, artist or type of ambient music you want and this fan site will undoubtedly be of massive help. It's an archive of sounds too, which are available for Real Audio streaming.

Epsilon http://www.hyperreal.org/music/epsilon
An information archive which links to most of the key ambient artist and label sites. Simple as that.

Obsolete http://www.obsolete.com
Stylishly presented links for many ambient and techno labels and bands.

Anti-sites

The Beatles http://www.he.net/
Suck Homepage ~excelsior/beatles
Ranting. Mainly about Ringo.

I Hate Mariah http://www.oe-pages.com/ARTS/RB/mariahpooh
Boy, there are some sick people out there. And on http://entermam.tripod.com you will find another person who isn't keen on her, either.

Boy Bands Suck http://www.angelfire.com/ny3/boybandssuck
Little more need be said.

Artists A-Z

A1   http://www.a1-online.com

A flashy site for the popular young boys – all spinning logos and beautifully reproduced photographs. The music's not bad, either.

Abba   http://www.abbasite.com

Official and definitive, complete with Real Audio and video clips, biographies and pictures of everyone involved in the making and marketing of this band. Whew! Check out Stig Anderson's head! The joy of this site is that it treats Abba as a band, not as the kitsch, retro, marketing concept that some people mistake them for.

Aerosmith   http://www.aerosmith.com/Hi/index.html

Hi-tech and definitive, but we could do with a few more audio-visual bits, please, guys.

Christina Aguilera   http://www.christina-a.com

Her official website is yet again more proof that teen pop stars seem to be producing the best fan resources: up-to-date news, pix and sound clips. The US record company on http://www. peeps. com/christina offers a lot of exclusive Real Time video out-takes from the 'Genie in a Bottle' video and other good fan-related content.

Air   http://source.astralwerks.com/air

Full of downloads, audio streams and cool images, this is a perfect accompaniment to the French duo's sophisticated ambient pop.

Alice in Chains   http://www.aliceinchains.net/splash-f.html

Occasionally fun, but mainly dreary archives of news and negativity.

Tori Amos   http://tori.by.net

The best place to go for everything on this piano-straddling star is the fan-run Dent In The Tori Amos Net Universe, which truly has it all. Cornflake City, another unofficial site at **http://www.geocities. com/SunsetStrip/Lounge/**1826**/main.html** is also really good for news, and the official site on **www.http://tori.com** is not bad, either.

The Artist   **http://www.love4oneanother.com**
Formerly known as Prince, that is. This is the official site. Just one song on it. Less is … less.

Backstreet Boys   **http://www.backstreetboys.com**
Groovy, with lots of in-depth information on all the band members and beautiful pix.

Basement Jaxx   **http://www.astralwerks.com/basementjaxx**
If only this matched the frenzied excitement of the band's records or shows. The graphics are cool and funky, but this is way too light in content.

Bay City Rollers   **http://users.aol.com/buesken/bcr/bcr.htm**
The host, Gerd Büskens, tells us more than we really need to know about the betartaned lads with the unfortunately mouthed drummer. Oh, they sang 'Shangalang' as they ran with the gang – not the Crips or the Bloods, we hasten to add.

Beach Boys   **http://www.beachboysfanclub.com**
Each Boy is given the proper treatment on this reverential Fan Club page.

Brian Wilson   **http://www.cabinessence.com/brian**
Fantastic and all-encompassing, with hundreds of links (each with an accurate description) to the many Beach Boys sites out there. Check out the chords to 'God Only Knows'!

Leonard Cohen   **http://www.serve.com/cpage/LCohen**
Bird On A Wire is the collected interviews, articles, reviews and musings of the poet/singer, plus all his words and music.

Beastie Boys http://www.beastieboys.com
Always striving to be ahead of the pack, these perennial hipsters come up trumps with this, their second, proper site. Expect everything you could hope for, plus the whole of the back catalogue available for MP3 download to compile your own Greatest Hits.

Beck http://www.beck.com
Quirky graphics and moving icons with the futuristic-retro feel that only artists like Beck and maybe the Beastie Boys can get away with. Best is 'In the studio', featuring audio and video streams from his work in progress. Great fun and a must for fans and non-fans alike.

Bee Gees http://www.columbia.edu/~brennan/beegees
Well-written fan site with so many links. Try the impressive official one, too, on http://www.beegees.net.

Captain Beefheart http://www.beefheart.com
Not just the man and his music, but also 100 of his paintings, beautifully scanned and catalogued. A site worthy of the underground genius.

Belle & Sebastian http://www.jeepster.co.uk/belleandsebastian
Very well put together with everything for fans of these award-winning indie darlings: up-to-date news, press photos, biogs, etc., plus idiosyncrasies such as poetry and fiction pages.

B*witched http://www.b-witched.com
The official Sony site and very good it is, too, with all the biogs, pix and music you want, plus a load of other blarney. The 'Cat Fact' feature will make you laugh.

Billie http://c3.vmg.co.uk/billie
All the teen sensation info, music, video-feeds and answered

questions you need straight from the mouth of the record company.

Björk   http://www.bjork.co.uk
Web Sense is a lovely, friendly place to which only this strange squeaky-voiced chanteuse could take us. Once you arrive, you are greeted by your host, Meester Fly, who guides you about in his own inimitable style. Download the videos, read about the past, present and future, and link all over. So cool the merchandise page is called 'Therapy'.

Blondie   http://www.blondie.ausbone.net/
A superb, unofficial Blondie resource with some great features like home-drawn cartoons on http://www.blondie.ausbone.net/pics/cartoon.jpg.

Blur   http://www.blur.co.uk
Official and minimal, this is tastefully produced and good-looking but does not contain anything that the average Blur fan won't have, or already know. The news mainly consists of telling us about things to buy. The people behind Blurb, the official Blur fan club, offer http://www.seething-prod.com/BFC, where you can find exclusive interviews and chat once you have registered with them.

Marc Bolan   http://www.mauloa.com/marcbolan/index.html
'Super Links' is a great place to start looking for the masses of Bolan stuff on the web, including the Official Marc Bolan Fan Club on http://www.marc-bolan.com/images/StuStar.gif who advise us to 'Keep a little Marc in our heart'.

David Bowie   http://www.davidbowie.com
Saatchi-sponsored modern art, interactive MP3 technology, all the latest Bowie.net news in cool graphics and a link to Dave's

artwork on http://www.bowieart.com Check out the fan sites in Chapter 6 too.

Boyzone   http://www.boyzone.co.uk
Not the best-looking site considering this is their official one, but certainly everything you could possibly to want to know about the boys, save their home addresses. But true fans always seem to find those out anyway.

Garth Brooks   http://www.simplygarth.com
Simply Garth covers pretty much everything about the country music superstar including links to his alter-ego Chris Gaines's page (http://www.chrisgaines.com).

Ian Brown   http://www.ianbrown.co.uk
Impressive official site from the gurning vocalist.

James Brown   http://www.funky-stuff.com
Funky Stuff is brilliant, informed and lovingly compiled, with separate entries for Maceo, Fred Wesley and Bootsy Collins. Bus driver, take it to the bridge!

Kate Bush   http://www.gaffa.org
Gaffaweb is the best place for Kate on the web: interviews, articles, reviews, archives, audio, video, a chat room – looks so stylish, too. Check out a couple of others in Chapter 3. Wow.

Buzzcocks   http://www.buzzcocks.com
Still going, still modern, and still missing Howard Devoto. Badum badum.

Mariah Carey   http://www.sonymusic.com/artists/MariahCarey
Courtesy of Sony, this has a fairly impressive bundle of goodies and is the place to go and get chatting about the decade's most

successful female solo artist. Her Official Fan Site on http://www.mariahcarey.org is unimaginative and quite dull.

Coal Chamber http://www.mysti.com/coalchamber
Piercings galore from the cartoonish gods of goth metal.

The Corrs http://www.corrsonline.com/
Corr! Even the drummer's attractive! Music, reviews, a chat room, photos and videos. Everything you want from the Corrs and a lot more than you're offered by the extremely disappointing official US record company site at http://www.atlantic-records.com/the_corrs.

Crosby, Stills, Nash & Young http://www.csny.net
Very fine indeed, this comes complete with a Pete Frame family tree – a very necessary inclusion for such a complex web of interrelated group activity. Every album is track-listed, and there is a bulletin board for fans, plus an online store.

Sheryl Crow http://www.sherylcrow.com
Nice to see a solo artist devoting a chunk of her website to the backing band. There is a news section with little actual news, but a charming tour diary and some good pictures. You can also join the Fan Forum if you so wish.

Daft Punk http://www.daftpunk.com
Massively stylish French outfit offer a site that, majesty-wise, is only a short promenade away from their music.

D'Angelo http://www.okayplayer.com/dangelo/interface.htm
Disappointing, considering the strength of this artist.

Def Leppard http://www.defleppard.com
A bit flabby but loads of links for anyone still interested in the (like Shania Twain) Mutt Lange-inspired lords of poodle-head rock.

Depeche Mode   http://www.depechemode.com
Black. Very black. And takes so long to load. When it's finally on
the screen it's a useful news resource and contains all the choice
items about the Mode you would want, were you a fan. Which we
all are, aren't we?

The Doors   http://www.elektra.com/rock_club/doors/
From the record company, this offers great links to some of the
hundreds of other Doors sites. They even give away sound files.
Cheers, Elektra! Try also http://www.thedoors.com, which is official
and very impressive, now updated for its second anniversary.

Nick Drake http://www.algonet.se/~iguana/DRAKE/DRAKE.html
With every scrap of the latest news, plus guitar tablature and
pictures, the 'Nick Drake Files' is the best choice from many pages
on the tragic yet hip-once-more folk hero.

Dr Dre   http://www.dre2001.com
As long as you've got the Shockwave software this is one sexy site:
every page is accompanied by the man's music and superb high-
quality moving graphics, plus all the other stuff that normal
websites consider boundary-breaking. The chronic.

Bob Dylan   http://www.bobdylan.com
A tremendous website – all the Grumpy One's albums divided up
by decade, each track available as a Real Audio clip, and detailed
liner notes you don't even get with the CDs themselves. As well as
this, there is a comprehensive lyric archive and a frequently
updated news section, and the whole thing looks great.

Elastica   http://www.stutter.demon.co.uk
A good, chock-a-block site which peters out towards the end of
1997. It doesn't seem to be getting any attention from the band
now, who claim to be too busy. Blimey, what are they doing?

Eminem   http://www.eminem.com
All the great videos, plus Real Audio streams of the album tracks.
A shame Mr Shady couldn't have taken some website hints from
his mate Dr Dre, but he was probably too busy hiding from his
mum.

Fatboy Slim   http://www.skint.net/artists/fbs/index.html
A surprising amount of text, and little of the frenetic activity you
would expect from the Cook man. Each release gets a write-up,
and the superb videos (Including Spike Jonze's 'Praise You') are
available to check out via Real Video.

Bryan Ferry/Roxy Music   http://www.dlc.fi/~hope/main.htm
Tired of the tango? Fed up with fandango? Bored with the
beguine? Then this is your scene.

5IVE   http://www.5ive.co.uk
Absolutely great official site from one of the best boy bands around;
good-looking, full of interesting features and easy to access – the
site, that is, not the band. Personal messages from the guys too.

Garbage   http://garbage.rlc.net
Fabulous-looking and modern; check out the merchandise section.
Mum! I want a 'Paranoid' condom! There's all the up-to-date news,
as well as music and messages from the band to audio-stream.

Macy Gray   http://www.macygray.com
Has a few video downloads for 'I Try', a personal letter from the
artist herself and a short-story competition. This last idea, as well as
fans getting asked to choose what the next Mace single should be,
helps create a more interactive feel.

Geri Halliwell   http://www.geri-halliwell.com
The Ginger One's official homepage has the distinction of splitting
the screen into 12 separate windows, yes that's right, 12 – all of

them making up the usual selection of biog, news, pix, audio, video and fan club stuff. Don't forget to close all the windows before you go out.

Deborah   http://www.primenet.com/
Harry   ~lab/deborahharry.html
Award-winning – a must for fans.

Jimi Hendrix   http://www.jimi-hendrix.com/magazin
Experience Hendrix is edited for Hendrix's estate by the man who used to run the independent site Digital Voodoo on http://www.lionsgate.com/music/hendrix. Both are brilliant.

Lauryn Hill   http://www.lauryn-hill.com
A little corporate for one allegedly so down-with-the-street; this does offer tiny audio clips for each Miseducation album track. Lyrics too.

Hole   http://www.holeonline.com
Official website. One would expect some pictures of Courtney here. Why not? They're everywhere else. Very content-light.

Natalie Imbruglia   http://www.imbruglia.com
The Almost Official Website is pretty definitive: great photo-scans, all the rumours absent from the official sources, and a great news section. The official site, http://www.natalie-imbruglia.co.uk, is useful too, if you want to know her shoe size and age. You don't, do you?

Michael Jackson   http://www.neverland.dk3.com
Neverland is basic-looking but absolutely rammed with content like up-to-date news, pictures, links, plus games and competitions.

Jamiroquai   http://www.jamiroquai.co.uk
Not a lot of content but modern and sexy with some great screensavers, some nice pix, and a 'Globetrotter' feature allowing us to map the Cat in the Hat's touring schedule.

Tom Jones   http://www.tomjones.com

The most up-to-date place keep up with the Jones boy. News in all European languages, and good coverage of all the Tight-Trousered One's past triumphs.

Kiss   http://www.kissonline.com

'The site that clicks ass'. Makes most other artist websites look like shopping lists scribbled on postcards.

Korn   http://www.korn.com

A powerful intro leads to all the usual expensive bumf – which is OK, but there are better areas to hunt for Korn, like http://www.kornweb.com/index.phtml, which won an Artist Direct Award for Best Rock fansite.

Kraftwerk   http://www.kraftwerk.com

If you have Flash-Shockwave, you're in for a treat. Animated old-school German graphics and sounds. Not much on it, but then minimalism always was the watchword with these boys. *Ein echtes Geschenk* for fans.

Kylie   http://www.kylie.com/kylieultra.html

Ultra is still one of the best artist websites around, not least for the overall three-dimensional feel of it and the winningly perverse 'Dress Kylie' feature.

Ladysmith Black Mambazo   http://www.mambazo.com

A wonderful and idiosyncratic resource – you can even learn Zulu here. Not a lot of people know that.

The   http://ourworld.compuserve.com/
Levellers   homepages/Mike_Walker/Leveller.htm

Tabs, chords, photographs and the sneaking feeling that you're doing something good by coming to this shrine to the much-maligned and newly scrubbed and shaven ex-crusties. There are also many links to good causes and action groups – the Levellers being one of the very, very few bands who said they were trying to change the world, and then actually tried to change the world. Good on them.

The Lilac Time   http://www.cookingvinyl.com/lilac/index.html
Charming site for Stephen Duffy's ongoing fraternal folk project. The history and background are engagingly written, the links are definitive and there are Real Audio samples too.

Limp Bizkit   http://www.limp-bizkit.com
Really impressive, all-shouting, all-moshing resource from the Bizkit men.

Jennifer Lopez   http://www.jenlopezfan.net
This fan network offers great place to find the latest news, plus a chat room, audio and, perhaps most importantly, pictures. Also worth looking at is the equally fun official site http://www. jenniferlopez.com/ie_index.html. Out of sight.

Madonna   http://www.madonnanet.com/mland
Hosted by the Madonna Network with frequently updated news and great links and features, this is essential for all Madonna fans. You could also have a look at the fan club page on http:// www.madonnafanclub.com, which is good for news but there are no exclusive pictures. For these try http://home.swipnet.se/ madonna/pages1.jpg – an amazing catalogue of rare, and often saucy, photos.

Manic Street Preachers   http://www.manics.co.uk
Designed for fans who want the usual pictures, news and video clips, this a solid effort from the Blackwood boys. No links to some of the more thoughtful and interesting fan sites, though.

Marilyn Manson   http://marilynmanson.net

Initially you are confronted with the quasi-religious imagery of a homepage linking to sites such as Frank's Pit of Eternal Darkness, Betty Bowers – America's Best Christian, and Deathscenes.com, but, hey, no Manson. The mascara'd little tease makes it a challenge to find him, but, once you have, this is modern, fun and full of surprises. Worth visiting even if you think his appeal wanes once you reach 16.

Dean Martin   http://www.deanmartinfancenter.com

My mother-in-law doesn't need glasses – she drinks straight out the bottle. Wonderful stuff. That is, as they say, *amore*.

Ricky Martin   http://www.rickymartinmanagement.com

A great news section, an adventurous library of photos, and a hint of the Latin feel the artist deserves, this is La Vida Loca compared with the official record company site, http://www.rickymartin. com, which is basic and a little sober for such an exotic and electric performer. Now, is he or isn't he?

Massive Attack   http://the-raft.com/massive/index.mezz.html

Unusually corporate, and takes ages to get nowhere. Also, it is sponsored by a well-known make of jeans – surely a career mistake?

Meatloaf   http://www.meatloaf-oifc.com

Well laid out, packed with superb pictures of Meat, and a real sense of fun.

Megadeth   http://www.megadeth.com

You will age prematurely while it loads, but it's pretty definitive when it finally arrives. Now, into the lungs of hell with you!

Metallica   http://www.encycmet.com

Encyclopaedia Metallica is a superb resource for all fans; clearly, almost clinically laid out, bang up to date and healthily aggressive.

George Michael   http://www.planetgeorge.org

Planet George claims to be the largest private fan site on the web and even offers a choice of the man's music to listen to while you browse. It is better than both the official resource, **http://eden. vmg.co.uk/georgemichael**, which is hard to navigate, and Aegean, **http://www.aegean.net**, which details things a little better, but has a layout mirroring Andrew Ridgeley's post-Wham! career. Messy.

Missy Elliott   http://www.missy-elliott.com

Typically smart site from the queen of two-step garage. Plenty of misdemeanour, and ample evidence that she's a bee-atch.

Joni Mitchell   http://www.jonimitchell.com

The best Mitchell resource, cataloguing most of her career – including scans of her impressive art.

Moby   http://www.moby.org

A fan site that's just about the definitive word on the US artist's close-shaven career. Check out the sizeable image bank.

Mogwai   http://www.mogwai.co.uk

NME-recommended site for the Scottish post-rock faves.

Alanis Morissette   http://www.maverickrc.com/alanis

For fans, this is the best place to start looking for the web's alleged Most Popular Artist. It has RealAudio clips, an up-to-date news section and masses of links. The star's own page **http://www. alanismorissette.com** is not as professional and extensive, but it has an appealing quirkiness, and once you are a member there are many fun things to do on the paintbox page and occasional free MP3 downloads. Reprise Records' **http://www.repriserec.**

com/alanis looks good but is utterly devoid of any content whatsoever, save a constant mantra-like banner on every vacuous page asking you to 'buy this album?' No.

Van   **http://www.harbour.sfu.ca/**
Morrison   **~hayward/van/van.html**
Definitive site for the man with the throat of gravel, the soul of an angel and the tolerant nature of a billy goat with a migraine.

Youssou-N'Dour   **http://w3.to/youssou-ndour**
Unofficial page offering sound streams and news, with links to other information resources.

Nine Inch Nails   **http://www.nin.com**
Trent Reznor makes his site difficult to deal with but fun all the same. Not unlike his albums, really. For more information-based sites try http://www.nineinchnails.net/news and http://members.xoom.com/ninarchive.

N'Sync   **http://www.gurlpages.com/music/nsync_4-ever1/**
As good as it gets for the handsome pop fellas. One of the many fan sites that go through Gurl Pages, a sort of fans' *Just 17/Sassy* online.

Oasis   **http://www.oasisnet.com**
The 21st-century Slade offer a meat-and-potato site for their fan base. Visually dull and missing any real content other than information on how to spend your cash on their concert tickets. Far from Supersonic. Check out Chapter 6 for something less insulting.

Orbital   **http://www.loopz.co.uk**
NME-recommended page from the shaven-headed techno heroes. The news scrolls upwards automatically allowing us to choose

a piece, the video downloads are tremendous and the text is well written.

Pavarotti   http://www.deccaclassics.com

Follow the links from the record company's homepage to find a biography of the great man, some nice photographs and a tour schedule. If you're a fan you could check out his own site http://www.lucianopavarotti.it although it is not particularly user-friendly. The big man sells his performance tickets here but offers little else besides a few biographical details. You'd expect something a little ... well, fatter.

Pavement   http://www.pavementtherockband.com

This is a fairly standard official band site, with added exclusive live recordings in streamed audio. There is also some concert footage and all the band's videos to watch.

Phish   http://www.phish.com

E-music's number-one act for MP3 downloads are big in all areas. The band's site, while not really being a playground for fans, is frank and practical. Don't buy tickets from scalpers!

Pink   http://ourworld.compuserve.com/
Floyd   homepages/PFArchives

There are masses of Floyd websites out there – this lists most of them.

Syd Barrett   http://www.pink-floyd.org/barrett

Everything you need to know about the man and the cult around him, including MP3s.

Public Enemy   http://www.public-enemy.com

Famous for making the group's last album, There's a Poison Goin' On, available online before Def Jam got it to the stores, this is not just a website: it's a political statement.

Elvis Presley   http://www.elvis-presley.com
The only web presence authorised by Elvis Presley Enterprises Inc.,
it does give us the joy of listening to the King in Real Audio while
we browse, but we have to tolerate being given the hard sell on
rooms in the Elvis Presley Heartbreak Hotel and tables at the
Memphis Restaurant with its 'Authentic Southern Hospitality'.

The Prodigy   http://www.prodigy.co.uk
Right now, the complete Real Video version of the once shocking
'Smack My Bitch Up' seems a tad tired. This site no doubt will be
updated once the Prodge get round to doing some new stuff.

Puff Daddy   http://www.puffdaddy.com/
Are you calling my website a Puff? Well, it really isn't up to much
considering the enormity of this biz-player. With links to his label
on http://www.badboyonline.com, this is hi-tech, state-of-the art
and good looking, but light in content; his lifestyle magazine
Notorious, which initially seems like a great link, turns out to be just
an advert for us to take out a subscription.

Radiohead   http://www.radiohead.com
Absolutely one of the finest sites available on the web. Exclusive
photos and artwork, Colin's diary (http://www.radiohead.
com/colin.html), thought-provoking slogans, masses of surprising
links – all presented in unique stylish graphics. Even if you are not a
fan, it is worth visiting for the sheer unpredictability and bravado.

Rage Against the Machine   http:www.//ratm.com
Alternative album covers, clips of 'Killing In the Name Of' and other
hits during your browsing. You can also choose the news you read:
Rage updates or general politics. Admirable and worthy.

The Red Hot Chili Peppers   http://www.redhotchilipeppers.com
A grandiose front page stating 'Rockinfreakapotimous Presents'

gives way to the standard set of destinations such as news, pictures, music clips and merchandise. Good for fans.

Lou Reed   http://www.loureed.org
Lou's official website is scarily organised and great-looking – all flashing icons and dark imagery. The news page is frequently updated, the links are definitive and the Timeline biography is superb.

REM   http://www.remhq.com
Official, but like the Radiohead site, this feels as if it had been done by the band themselves, who claim to be the last group in the known world to have a website. Tell that to poor old Bum Gravy.

Todd Rundgren   http://www.tr-i.com
Done by Todd, himself, and jolly good fun it is, too. No, really.

The Rolling Stones   http://www.the-rolling-stones.com
The familiar, almost comforting Andy Warhol tongue logo appears as a first image, giving way to great content such as games called 'Which Riff Is It?' and 'Build A Bridge To Babylon', and exclusive clips from the recent tour – Keith looking better in Real Time video-clip form than he does in real life. Waiting for the downloads reminds you of Charlie Watts's comment about life with the band being five years rockin' and 20 years hanging around for Mick. Try also http://www.stones.com, which is unofficial but very professional.

The Runaways http://www.ite.his.se/%7Ec95chrha/secrets.html
The band that spawned Joan Jett and the Blackhearts, plus thousands of imitation hard-rock girl groups.

Santana   http://www.santana.com
Official resource for the Latin guitar hero still wowing the punters in the US charts after over 30 years. Includes set lists and equipment

features for the would-be Carlos. No, no that Carlos – international terrorists need not apply.

Savage Garden   http://www.savagegarden.com
News-packed, content-rich and stylish official site from the Brisbane duo.

S Club 7   http://www.sclub7.co.uk
Very impressive, with both US and UK content. Best to load up with Flash before you start so you can appreciate the cool graphics and sounds. A superb example of just what can be achieved with a little thought and care.

Silver Chair   http://www.chairpage.com
They kick off by wishing all the best to an ailing David Letterman. Is this really rock 'n' roll, guys? One of them is going out with Natalie Imbruglia, so we can't possibly like them.

Sepultura   http://www.sepultura.com.br
The Brazilian hard rockers, minus their founder and leader Max Cavalera (now with Soulfly), give fans a place to find out where the action is.

Simply Red   http://www.simplyred.co.uk
If you are a fan of the band then you may enjoy a brief visit here, but there is little real content and a disturbing number of photos of Mick. If you're not a fan, then you could do worse than check out the hilarious 'Mick Hucknall's Pink Pancakes' on http://www.ntk. net/tvgohome/170999.html.

Frank Sinatra   http://www.nj.com/sinatra/gif/upperleft.gif
'The Voice From Hoboken NJ', which is fan-run, is absolutely great. The Reprise years were not his very best but http://www. repriserec.com/sinatra/index.html is worth a look.

Skunk Anansie   http://the-raft.com/skunk/index.html
The shouty, shaven-headed politico-rockers offer an official place
to find live webcasts and exclusive photos.

Slipknot   http://www.slipknot1.com
The commanding intro page, http://www.slipknot2.com/
preview2000.htm, is worth visiting alone. This is a site with a major
attitude. If you don't have Shockwave, though, try the great fan
page 'Killers Are Quiet' on http://members.tripod.com/~zzcrowzz

Will Smith   http://www.willsmith.net
This takes a while to load up but, once installed, it offers a great
variety of Shockwave-spiced Willennium news and pictures.

Britney Spears   http://www.britneyspearsfans.com
Her Official Fan Club Site is one of the most hi-tech and impressive
around and worth visiting even if you can't bear thinking about the
ubiquitous teen siren. The record company's site at http://
www.peeps.com/britney/ is solid, if a little stolid, with pictures,
videos, info and a beautiful pink background. Her official site,
http://britneyspears.com, has clips from the videos, a chance to
'Show Me a Sign!' (ie email her) but, sadly, nowhere in evidence
are those infamous Rolling Stone photos.

Spice Girls   http://c3.vmg.co.uk/spicegirls/nowspice
This official Virgin C3 site is packed with impressive audio and video
streams and concert video footage – colourful, well put together
and fast. Just like the girls. The official US resource,
(http://www.virginrecords.com/newspice) while having some
great pictures, is a little out of date though.

Melanie C   http://www.northern-star.co.uk
Fairly minimal, covering the burgeoning solo career of the
annoyingly ubiquitous and apparently rock-loving Sporty.

Steps　　　　　　　　　　　　http://www.gensteps.co.uk

This award-winning unofficial location has all the bits you would expect from a grown-up website – really up-to-date news, pictures and a chat room, plus goodies such as all the Steps' dance routines mapped out. It is so much better than the official US record company site http://www.peeps.com/steps, which just has some pleasant photos and a few video clips.

Stereophonics　　　　　　　　http://www.stereophonics.co.uk

Solid and reliable, like the band, this site reflects their hard-working and fan-loyal attitude. The only downside is the news not being terribly up to date.

Sting　　　　　　　　　　　　http://www.stingchronicity.co.uk

Run in co-operation with Outlandos, Sting's only official fan club, this has accurate and up-to-date news and, in the absence of a proper record company site, it's the best. The tour site http://sting.compaq.com/flash.asp is very impressive visually and has frequently updated tour diaries from the man himself. A must for anyone with six-inch wooden plates shoved between their lips and teeth.

Suede　　　　　　　　　　　　http://www.suede.net

An international flavour for the boys, with news updates from Sweden and Holland appearing first. There is a biography, a shop and other stuff you would expect, but overall the feel is slightly clinical. Unsurprisingly, there are no Bernard Butler links.

Supergrass　　　　　　　　　http://www.supergrass.com

A really content-rich and quirky site, reflecting the nature of the band perfectly. Check out Micky Quinn's 'Children of the Monkey Basket' page at http://supergrass.densitron.net/index.html.

13th Floor Elevators   http://www.ed.brocku.ca/~paul/favorite/elevators

All about the seminal cult psychedelic band – great.

TLC   http://www.peeps.com/tlc

All the girls' efforts have obviously been focused on their music, judging from the lack of content here. A few scraps of info and some Real Video clips are pretty much it. Unpretty.

Tupac Shakur   http://www.tupacshakur.com

This is the official Tupac site and it's a homepage, a tribute and shrine to a remarkable talent cut off in his prime. Either that or a rapper who flirted with violence once too often and got burned. Or both. This site, naturally, takes the former stance.

Shania Twain   http://www.shania.com

Much like the genre-defying singer's music, this site can't settle on a style and is a bit cluttered, but tasty all the same.

Type O Negative   http://www.roadrun.com/artists/TypeONegative

This is the official Roadrunner records page. For more Type-type try http://members.aol.com/daveburger.

U2   http://www.u2one.com

Well written and frequently updated, this fan resource is comprehensive, easy on the eye and about as close to an official website as you could want in the inexplicable absence of one.

The Verve   http://the-raft.com/theverve

Lovingly cared for and maintained, it claims, by the band. Looks brilliant and includes much exclusive stuff, such as an interview with the producer of Urban Hymns. The library of archived video, reviews and concert footage goes right back to the band's baggy years.

Westlife   http://www.westlife.co.uk

You have to go through an unbelievably complex safe-cracking exercise to get into the record company BMG's Backstage hub area. Once you're registered, a second, equally frustrating, search for Westlife results in a paltry list of their future engagements complete with postage-stamp-sized photograph. Laughable.

The Who   http://www.thewho.net

The fan-run The Hypertext Who is the best place to go for fans. The official store site is on http://thewhodirect.com which sells a lot of John Entwhistle's art. He has his own official site – on http://www.eden.com/theox – and so does Pete Townsend, on http://www.petetownshend.net/bitinga.gif where you can find, among lots of other things, useful advice on tinnitus.

Robbie Williams   http://www.robbiewilliams.co.uk

All the latest news, plus videos, live feeds and a gallery of everybody's favourite ex-member of Take That. Check out the 'Entertainer' section – must have been fun when they came up with that idea in the pub. Shame about the terrible blue and snot-green colour scheme.

Wu-Tang Clan   http://www.wu-tang.com

Two flashing icons lead to Wu Films and Bobby Digital, in turn leading to more amazing graphics, then music and video. This is truly state-of-the-art and, apart from taking a while to load, it is worth having a look at even if you are not a fan of Ol' Dirty Bastard, the RZA and their tough-guy mates. Not as hi-tech, but easier to navigate, and equally recommended, is the fan-page on http://www.geocities.com/SunsetStrip/Exhibit/7421/index.html.

Neil Young   http://hyperrust.org

Hyper Rust is the definitive Neil Young location. It contains absolutely everything you could possibly want, from a bibliography to the chords to 'Old Man'. All presented in a cool virtual notebook.

Frank Zappa   **http://zappa.com**
Maintained by the Zappa Estate itself, this is the big one, covering and documenting aspect of his career and a total must even for the most casual of fans. Rykodisc's is good, too, on **http://www. rykodisc.com/RykoInternal/Features/195/default.htm** – check out the bugs darting about the page as you scroll down.

Artwork

The Album Covers Page   **http://www.knl.com/albums**
Anything you want to see they can get via an enormous alphabetically ordered column of links. The front page contains a suspiciously large collection of sleeves from bands of the heavier-rock persuasion. But, hey, at least they always made more of an effort than blurred-out indie bands and grinning teenyboppers. So viva the Scorpions and Witchfinder General!

Cover   **http://freespace.virgin.net/**
Heaven   **love.day/coverheaven**
Record-cover art, plus an obsession with beautiful women on album sleeves. Electric Ladyland ahoy!

Covers   **http://covers.virtualave.net**
Customise your wallpaper with album covers from an impressive database.

Bhangra

Desi Sound   **http://www.desisound.com**
Great for Asian music fans: a frequently updated news section, clear layout plus Real Audio clips from current favourites.

Bhangra.Com　　　　　　　　**http://www.bhangra.com**
Loads of MP3s to download, plus a chat room.

The Beatles

Abbey Road　　　　　　**http://www.abbeyroad.co.uk/**
Studios　　　　　　　　　　　　　　**indexam.html**
Go to the fun page on this industry site from the world's most famous recording studio and you too can leave graffiti all over the walls outside.

Beatlefest　　　　　　　　　**http://www.beatlefest.com**
Frequently updated for Beatle-related news, this New Jersey homepage claims to have the world's largest Beatle mail-order catalogue.

Beatles　　　　　　　　　　**http://radiowavenet.com/**
Encyclopaedia　　　　　　　　**beatles/beatles.htm**
All the mop-tops' lyrics analysed to the last word.

Beatles Fans　　**http://beatles.about.com/entertainment/**
Index　　　　　　　　　　　**beatles/blalbums.htm**
About.com's Robert Fontenot attempts to document every single available Beatles link or story on the web ever, from 'Please Please Me' to 'Let It Be'. Give this man a day off.

Beatles Web　　**http://www.beatlesweb.co.uk/beatlemain.htm**
A fan page with up-to-date news and a good selection of photos. All this plus a comprehensive library of information on the Fabs' endlessly interesting life and times.

Blues

The Blue Highway　　　　**http://thebluehighway.com**
A superb resource – go there right now and soak up the authentic

Mississippi Delta atmosphere. No cussin' or spittin' in the chat room, though.

Blues World　　　　　　　　　http://www.bluesworld.com
Loads of links to fabulous-sounding hokey blues sites such as Rabbitt Brown – New Orleans songster, Sweet Pie Restaurant and Wilroy Sanders.

Calypso/Soca

Bajan Calypso Barn　　　　　　http://www.iere.com/thebarn
Archives of music and information from Antigua, Barbados, St Kitts, Jamaica and all over the Caribbean, covering not just calypso, but soca, katso, zouk and, er, chutney.

Calypso Tent of the Air　　　　　　http://www.kaiso.net
From Port of Spain, Trinidad, this is a superb place to find out about what is going on in this good-humoured, sunny genre – 'You will definitely not get a degree here, but you will certainly get a good education.' Like going on holiday.

Caribbean Festival　　　　　http://www.caribbeanfestival.org
You can discover everything you want to know about the eighth annual Festival of Caribbean Music from this resource run from the Bronx, New York. As well as this, it has masses of links, plus special pages, such as the one devoted to the Grenadian Calypsonian of the Century, the Mighty Sparrow on http://www.caribbeanfestival.org/mighty-sparrow.htm.

Lord Kitchener　　　　　　　　　http://www.intr.net/
Tribute　　　　　　　　　goyewole/kitchbd.html
The enormously influential Grandmaster of Calypso, known affectionately as 'Kitch' to legions of fans all over the world, died in February – this site is a tribute to his life and music.

Memory Lane   http://www.interlog.com/
Music   ~socagm/memorylane2/index.html
Proud Trinidadian George Maharaj welcomes us to the wonderful
world of calypso and steelpan music – this is a great place to start
looking for all things 'calypsonian'. Yes it is a word.

The Mighty Sparrow   http://www.mightysparrow.com
'Calypso King of the World' presents his own website, which offers
news, downloads and pictures, but has you skanking round the
room with impatience at the time it takes to load.

Socafusion   http://www.geocities.com/Hollywood/
         Highrise/5148/SOCAFUSION.htm
Promising to put, 'Soca in Yuh Head' with lots of MP3 downloads,
this is mind-bogglingly vast and ever expanding.

Trinidad Guardian   http://www.guardian.co.tt
Always loads of festival and music updates in this useful
newspaper site for the island.

Celtic

Celtic CD Clearance   http://www.cedarcottage.com
A bargain CD store for traditional music.

Celtic Music.Com   http://www.celticmusic.com
Focuses on Irish and Scottish music, and you can find loads of MP3s
here.

Ceolas Celtic Music Archive   http://www.ceolas.org/ceolas.html
Exhaustive and frequently updated Celtic music archive has everything from tons of links to the notation for well-known folk songs.

Coyne Celtic Imports   http://www.coyneceltic.com
Only in New York would a shop exist selling clothing and

equipment for pipe bands, bagpipe accessories and the instrument itself, plus the chance to have lessons yourself.

Kenny's Celtic and Folk   http://www.surfnetusa.com/
Music Reviews   celtic-folk
A very impressive archive of information from the boy Kenny, which divides its time between Irish music such as that of Mary Black and Brendan O'Loughlin and more general folk music such as Nick Drake and Kate Rusby.

Charities

You know, maybe it's time we started giving something back.

Rock The Vote   http://www.rockthevote.org
Well, after the Britpop-sponsored UK version that helped usher in Tony Blair, this US campaign now gears up for the presidential election and beyond. Educating American youth with the help of artists such as Wyclef Jean.

Classical

Bach Homepage   http://www.jsbach.org
If you love Bach, this is it. Get Bach! Get Bach!

BBC Music   http://www.bbcmusicmagazine.
Magazine   beeb.com
Reviews of classical CDs you can buy plus an up-to-date news channel, links to other classical-music resources and extremely literate reviews.

Classical Composers Poster   http://www.culturekiosque.com
Have a look at this superb timeline of every major composer.

Classical   http://www.igc.apc.org/
Music   ddickerson/-music.html

A vast library of links to some brilliant sites, all described in great detail, plus streamed audio to listen to while you browse.

Classical Music On The Web USA   http://classicalusa.com

A good place to start with resources such as a search engine and a library of reviews.

Classical Net   http://www.classical.net/music/search.html

A search resource with page upon page of composers, conductors, recommended recordings and event listings.

Culture Kiosque   http://www.culturekiosque.com

Truly European – it's in three languages – this general what's-on guide is very good for jazz and classical events news.

Georgetown   http://www.gprep.pvt.k12.md.us/
Classical Library   classical

A virtual library of classical music based at Georgetown prep school, biog manuscripts, and educational material.

Global Music Network   http://www.gmn.com

Hours of jazz and classical music, both to download and to stream, exclusive live audio and video webcasts, plus features and support information on composers and performers.

Mozart   http://www.classical.net/music/
     comp.lst/mozartwa.html

Classical Net's composer resource at http://www.classical.net/music/composer is one of the best on the web, as this page on Mozart shows.

Music Web UK   http://www.musicweb.uk.net

Very fast search engine for UK classical news and releases,

plus composer biographies, Real Audio, articles, interviews, CD reviews, a chat room, competitions and links – an impressive and meticulous site.

Vox Classical Music Shop　　　　　**http://www.voxcd.com**
A cheap New York shop, specialising in classical music.

Clubs and Clubbing

Clearly, in these rave-orientated days, there are far too many brilliant clubs for us to give you any more than the most basic selection. To ensure a bangin' night out, check out the more general sites. Many of the magazines in Chapter 4 regularly update their lists of clubs, and so there's no need for you to miss out wherever you are in the world.

Club Connexion　　　　　**http://www.clubconnexion.com**
Dividing the UK up into four regions, this finds the country's best clubs – links are provided if the club has its own site. The news is up to date and often essential, such as news of the dodgy drugs currently doing the rounds.

Club New York　　　　　**http://www.clubnyc.com**
A fully fledged magazine-style resource where you can do all your decision making online. It's aimed at busy Wall Street traders with little free time, but is useful for the tourist too. Punch in the Manhattan area you fancy, as well as the type of club you want to visit, and a list as long as your forthcoming bar bill will materialise.

Cream　　　　　**http://www.cream.co.uk**
You can get a weekly newsletter, or simply click on the news page of this beautifully presented site. Actually not a lot of content here and could do with a little music too.

The Fridge   **http://www.fridge.co.uk**

Andrew Czezowski's Brixton club goes online, where there is
everything you need to find out what is going on club- and bar-
wise – you can even listen to streamed samples of the music you
will be dancing to.

Los Angeles Bars   **http://weekendevents.com/**
and Dance Clubs   **LOSANGEL/lamusic.html**

Does just what it promises. Plan your boogying in advance.

Ministry Of Sound   **http://www.ministryofsound.com**

Impressively non-elitist dance webzine which is easy to navigate
offering lots of MP3s to download for free, plus the latest news,
informed reviews, pictures and listings of your favourite clubs and
its own radio station. Bangin'.

NYCE Clubs   **http://nyceclubs.com/clubs**

Not as extensive as Club New York but helpful in providing a map
allowing you to pinpoint exactly where it was that you punched
those two bartenders and got off with that truck driver from Ohio.
Hey, next time take your mother!

World Clubs Net   **http://www.worldclubs.net/**

Want to find a house club in Japan, or a bar in Melbourne playing
soul? A useful resource that sounds too good to be true, but
it really is all here. A couple of attempts resulted in finding some
clubs that made it sound worth catching the first plane to Tokyo.

Collectors

For extra rarities, signed items and all things vinyl, skip back to the
'Second-hand and collectables' section in Chapter 2.

eBay   **http://www.ebay.com**

This is a bit of a winner. Head for http://listing.ebay.com/aw/

listings/list and arrive directly at the music auction part of what
they describe as Your Personal Community Auction Site. John Barry
albums for $5 can't be bad.

Goldmine   http://www.krause.com/records/gm
The best magazine site for collectors.

Hits Under   http://www.icollector.com/
The Hammer   live/hits.htm
The largest online auction of music memorabilia ever; absolutely
fascinating – even if you don't want to get your wad out.

iCollector   http://www.icollector.com
I'm the iCollector, twisted iCollector. Actually there's not that much
music here. Growing though.

Recollections   http://www.recollections.co.uk
A mammoth A-Z of artists featuring all the legally available memo-
rabilia you could possibly desire, from Abba's autographs to ZZ
Top's shiny red vehicle.

Country

About   http://countrymusic.miningco.com/
Country   entertainment/countrymusic
About.com's country page is a good place to start looking for
country music links.

Country and Western   http://www.outofservice.
Song Generator   com/country
Click away to create such classics as 'She was breakin' out
with acne but I loved her and knew that she would be a crushing
bore ...'

Country Cool http://www.countrycool.com
Featuring a 28-56K stream of Internet radio, this resource is also a spot-on hoedown of news and information with updates on artists ranging from Billy Ray Cyrus to Wynonna Judd. Recommended.

Country Countdown http://www.top40countdown.com
Hosted by the perfectly monikered and hirsute Dan Steely, this site has much more than just a chart rundown: there are daily news updates, games and biographies, plus a choice of music on the jukebox.

Countrysong http://countrysong.com
A country music resource which, despite an out-of-date news section, contains a useful web guide for almost 200 country stars, a discussion forum and online radio broadcasts.

Country Stars http://www.countrystars.com
A webzine with masses of up-to-date news on everything that is going on in the world of country. It includes chat rooms and the occasional chance to talk to the big-hatted stars.

MCA Nashville http://www.mca-nashville.com
MCA's Nashville offshoot remains the best country label: get Flash installed, then sit back and enjoy a packed programme of fresh tracks, images and information from top contemporary artists such as Trish Yearwood, Mark Chestnutt and the current country superstar George Strait.

Music City News http://www.mconline.com
They were 'The Voice of County' but they are now sadly defunct. You can, however, get back issues of this great magazine from here.

Suite 101 Country   **http://www.suite101.com/**
and Western   **welcome.cfm/country_and_western**
An expert's guide to the genre with an overview and new plus links to some of the sites mentioned here and countless others.

Twang This   **http://www.twangthis.com**
Exclusive news and lots of other denim-shirted, big-booted hospitality from this site; from Martina McBride to Rebecca Lynn Howard and back to Merle Haggard, it is all here.

Dance

Dance Music Resource Pages   **http://www.juno.co.uk**
Updated weekly, with over 500 dance page links, this site features listings of all new UK dance releases, including catalogue numbers and distributor info, plus news of future releases and UK dance radio listings.

Dancesite   **http://www.dancesite.com**
Weekly updated full-length tracks available to audio-stream, well-written news and reviews, a genre guide (big beat or alternative dance?) to help avoid embarrassment in fashionable shops, and a search resource to help you find the music you want. Sorted.

Disquiet   **http://www.disquiet.com**
Packed with interviews and a superb discography of electronica books, this puts some brains behind the turntables.

Drum And Bass Arena   **http://www.breakbeat.co.uk**
Updated daily, this e-zine is a dense jungle of news, reviews and interviews.

Hyper Real   **http://www.hyperreal.org**
This dance culture site started in 1992, and continues to be original,

informed and interesting. Lots of frequently updated links to other sites too.

Kiss http://www.livesexy.co.uk

Like the Cream site, it looks great but not a lot is going on. It's pink, it's green, it's got a chat room where you can flirt. Cheers.

Motion http://motion.state51.co.uk

A really superb search resource for dance record shops worldwide – punch in the genre, the area and the country, and Bob could possibly be your UNKLE.

Pete Tong's Essential Selection http://essentialselection.com

Some exclusive Tong mixes which are updated every fortnight, but this site, which hovers midway between Tong's record-executive-for-London-Records day job and his DJ night job, leaves us wanting less self-promotion and more news, reviews and music.

Pyraplastic http://www.pyraplastic.com

Welsh drum and bass music producer offers underground record-production tips, links and samples.

Raya http://www.c8.com/raya

Website of the multimedia collective whose events mix music, visual and computer art and live performance. The site includes forthcoming-event listings as well.

Speed Garage http://www.speedgarage.com

Easy to understand with great links and audio files.

Street Sound http://ssound.pseudo.com

House music and electronica rule at this US site, which is more of an e-zine than a search resource. The content is different and genre-hopping (from Donald Byrd to UNKLE) and the look and atmosphere, though maybe a little dark, is professional and friendly.

X-Network   **http://www.x-network.co.uk**
A network of different resources, such as, for example,
http://www.doggin.net, a resource for DJs, or http://www.e-
clubbers.com, which is for, er, clubbers. Each directory is well
organised and clearly written. For instance, the drugs information
is accurate and scientific, without being scaremongering.

Dancing

Dancer.Com   **http://www.dancer.com/dance-links/**
A superb links source from ballet to jazz to break dancing.

Rocksteady   **http://www.ziplink.net/**
                                    ~upsetter/earnest/rock_steady.html
A deadly serious site on the mechanics of this very cool dance.

Skanking   **http://www.skaville.com/rudemoods/**
                                                  skankin/skankers.gif
There is a very limited amount of skanking info on the net, so the
gap is usefully filled by this extraordinary site. One step beyond!

Easy Listening

Blues Eyes.Com   **http://www.blue-eyes.com**
Arrive here and Frank Sinatra – evergreen Blues eyes himself – is
winkin' atcha. Possibly the best Sinatra tribute page and a genuine
pleasure to hang around in till the wee small hours.

Club Velvet   **http://www.tamboo.com**
A splendid Caribbean island theme to this easiest of Easy Listening
destinations. Fifties graphics, cocktail recipes and Kini's own huge
record collection. Swing it, daddio.

Hugh's Lounge In Foggy London http://www.users.dircon.co.uk
A bizarre virtual night out for fans of easy and exotica, includes
Herb Alpert and Esqivel – and a virtual dinner!

The Lounge Scene   http://www.geocities.com/Tokyo/3076
Smashing pink and white polka-dotted front page leading to the
romantically named Ariel Tagar's homepage. There are many links
and, though many of them work only inconsistently, they are all
appropriately tacky.

Swank-o-Rama   http://www.mindspring.com/
                                ~jpmckay/sound.html
'Dedicated to better living through cocktail culture'. You'd be hard
pushed to find an easier easy site. Hep cats.

Welcome To Vik's Lounge   http://www.chaoskitty.com
A totally bonkers easy-listening site with a ranting *maître d'* guiding
us round the host's madness. Inspired.

Folk

Folk Corporation   http://www.folkcorp.co.uk
Links to a selection of artists with a particular bias towards Fairport
Convention-related ones, such as the drummer Dave Mattacks
(who also played for Nick Drake).

Folk Music   http://www.folkmusic.org
Masses of venues listed for all your live date needs, plus a media
channel with some good video archives.

Folk Roots   http://www.froots.demon.co.uk
Charts, lists and reviews from the real-world magazine of the same
name, this is best regarded as an update source, rather than a
complete service in its own right.

Index of Folk   http://www..jg.org/folk

Packed with links to all the major players in this genre. This way for those keen on Pentangle.

World Folk Music Association   http://wfma.net

This homepage has a definitive artists index – Ralph McTell fans need look no further.

Hard Rock and Heavy Metal

Arguments still rage as to who started it. Was it Led Zeppelin, Black Sabbath, even the Yardbirds? But, whoever did it, heavy metal is clearly here to stay. In fact, it's everywhere – mixed in with glam, punk, rap, soul, industrial, goth ... you name it. Whatever and wherever it is, you'll probably find it at one of the addresses below.

About Heavy   http://heavymetal.about.com/
Metal   entertainment/heavymetal/mbody.htm

More expert guides by real experts. You need look no further than here for Twin Guitar Mayhem.

Anti MTV   http://www.antimtv.com

A metal directory focusing on bands, such as Slipknot, Deftones, NOFX and Incubus.

Black Velvet   http://www.blackvelvet.demon.co.uk

Glam meets punk in a fantastic, glossy, quarterly independent e-zine, stacked with pictures and news; the Manics meets the Sweet.

Classic Rock Daily   http://www.classicrockdaily.com

Lists of rock web-radio stations and up-to-date news of bass players in possession of the wrong sort of rocks. Focus is on less extreme alternative metal.

The Dark Site of Metal   http://metal.de
Also known as Metal-Online, this may be a struggle if your German
is weak, but, even without any linguistic skills, you will enjoy seeing
pictures of favourites such as Burden of Grief, Fleshcrawl, Mass
Hysteria, Kamelot, Sentenced and Sanity.

Extreme Music News   http://www.nestor.minsk.by/emn
MP3s, reviews and all the latest from artists such as the Kovenant,
Skeleton and Chainsaw Dismemberment.

Golden Age of   http://www.geocities.com/sunset/4001/
Rock and Roll   stome/the_golden_age.htm
A towering list of links to every group who may have conceivably
worn, or thought about wearing, make-up; Bad Religion to Bay
City Rollers to Buzzcocks, Joy Division to Jellyfish. Massive and
inspired.

Hard Rock Cafe   http://www.hardrock.com
A gallery of rock-'n'-roll artefacts, plus occasional webcasts.

Hard Rock   http://homes.acmecity.com/
Universe   music/metal/399
A one-stop for hard-rock and heavy-metal information; Korn to
Megadeth to Rage Against The Machine. Easy to navigate too.

KNAC online   http://www.knac.com/servlet/Index
The long-time standard for hard rock on the radio is now online,
but it is now a magazine as well and quite possibly the best of
its kind. A highlight is 'The Coroners Report', the weekly Death
Metal update.

Metal Edge Online   http://www.mtledge.com
Online magazine devoted to the hammer of the gods, but with a
$4.95 subscription they might be on a stairway to nothing.

Metal Hammer   http://www.metalhammer.co.uk
In the absence of a Kerrang! site this should be great, but it is inconsistent. You need to register for it too, so boo!

Metal Links   http://www.metallinks.com
UK-based A-Z of bands and labels – this is a useful resource but watch out for broken links.

Northern UK's Metal Page   http://www.shipley.ac.uk/north
Packed full of northern goodness such as labels, studios and resources, plus masses of local bands not exclusively for local people.

Peaceville   http://www.peaceville.com
Obscure and intriguing metal bands galore. Check out the latest on My Dying Bride, Opeth and Katatonia – Swedish Gods of Disharmony.

Doug Powell   http://members.home.net/musickle/doug.html
Who is he? No idea, but it doesn't matter, his site is brilliant fun.

Rock 108 from Key J   http://www.keyj.com
Fans of Metallica, Korn, Godsmack, Filter, Limp Bizkit and Creed need look no further for the full information, news and radio service.

Rock and Roll Hall of Fame   http://www.rockhall.com
Based in Cleveland, Ohio, the Hall of Fame offers a good place to visit on the web too: A 'Today In Rock' feature with birthdays and events plus details and illustrations of their exhibitions and useful links.

Rock and   http://www.rockworld.
Heavy Metal Page   ndirect.co.uk
UK-based site with a fairly traditional selection of vintage bands

with two words in their names, the first of which the true fan is usually obliged to omit – Lizzy, Priest, Sabbath, Zeppelin, etc.

Russian Darkside   **http://www.darkside.ekort.ou**

A trifle slow, but worth checking out to see what the devil is going on in the world of Russian death metal. Now there's a genre. Fascinating.

Slitzine   **http://www.geocities.com/ sunsetstrip/palms/4001/index.htm**

Californian punk rock from this glam-punk e-zine – they wear mascara, they're messed up and they're very, very loud.

Tombstone   **http://www.tombstone.gr**

Modestly barking that it is 'The Best Heavy Metal Fanzine on the Web', this monthly is definitely worth a look, particularly for the MP3s on offer.

UK Metal   **http://www.geocites.com/sunsetstrip/**
Underground   **palladium/9133/main.htm**

Aside from the infuriating GeoCities advert banners, which clog every page, this is a good place to visit and find an exhaustive list of links to great metal fansites.

Hip-hop

Atomic   **http://www.atomicpop.com/**
Pop   **aboutatomicpop/index.html**

A hip-hop shop with attitude to spare; MP3s to buy, including PE releases.

Boomshaka Music   **http://www.boomshakamusic.com**

Featuring Real Audio and Real Video feeds, and behind-the-scenes exclusives, Boomshaka focuses primarily on US urban music with a smattering of alternative. The layout is clear and easily navigable, even if the content is currently a little light.

Hip Hop Site   http://www.hiphopsite.com
Excellent online magazine with loads of great hip-hop release news, downloads, audio streams and links to other related pages. Some artists, such as Eminem, have sites that are affiliated to them.

The Source   http://thesource.tunes.com/sections/home
Massive database of everything you wanted to know about US hip-hop with up-to-date news too.

Humour

Band O Matic   http://www.joescafe.com/bands
Follow simple instructions to create band names from the random generator. School lunch break will never be the same again when you can sit around, coming up with stuff like Celebrity Ass Children and Sprouts Will Kill You Now.

Bluffers Guide   http://www.knopfler.com/Bluffers.html
David Knopfler's guide; witty, irreverent and fun.

Celebrity Death   http://www.seemslikesalvation.
Match   com/celeb_deathmatch
Trent Reznor versus Puffy Combs. Satisfying.

Claymation Spice Girls   http://clayvision.net/spice
Have a peek at pregnant Posh. Made of clay. Slightly more expressive than the real thing, then.

Exploding Geri   http://home.ptd.net/~omega/spice.html
Poof! Simple as that. What wouldn't Scary Spice give to have this be real?

Faeces Of The World   http://www.byrne.dircon.co.uk/faeces
Liam Gallagher or Michael Jackson: Warp them! Bend them! Mess them!

Hamster Dance   http://www.peermusic.com/cubanboys.html
Links to all that hamster business. Richard Gere's favourite. Oh, no, that was a gerbil.

The Lego Street Preachers   http://lsp.fortunecity.co.uk
Worth it for the album sleeves alone – 'Everything Lego', the 'Legoly Bible' etc.

Mini   http://freespace.virgin.net/
Pops   craig.robinson1/fminipopsx.html
Fantastic and totally original, this allows you to have a look at your favourite artists in minute comic-strip form – everyone from Steps to Spinal Tap.

Chris Morris   http://www.rethink.demon.co.uk/laugh.html
Music parodies and other bilious humour from the creator of *Brass Eye* and *The Day Today*. This is the news!

Mullets   http://www.mulletsgalore.com
Tear-jerkingly funny site devoted to the hairstyle of the devil. Def Leppard, White Lion, Great White, Joey Tempest ... Er, can we go home now?

Pulp Fiction Simpsons   http://www.jinxworld.com/bonus.htm
Just for the sheer heck of it, the Simpsons team did these sketches around the time Tarantino's seminal movie was released. Dick Dale's psychotic twanging accompanies your scroll down as you see all your favourite Simpsons characters re-enact famous scenes from the Pulp Fiction movie.

Rock School   http://www.rockschool.com

An absolutely terrific animated site. Load up with Shockwave and away you go; lessons on how to be a rock star, advice on everything from song writing to pulling the opposite sex. The Jamometer is pure genius, with 26 different licks to try out over a rocking beat. Go on, you know you want to.

Rutles   http://www.getback.org/rutles

Lovingly crafted site for the lovingly crafted Beatles pastiche, it documents the rise of the pre-fab four and details their recent reunion gigs. It moost be loove.

Scratch It   http://www.turntables.de.

'Are You Ready?!!!' Completely pointless and of course utterly brilliant, this is a time-waster in a league of its own: guide your mouse over two turntables and a microphone and create your own scratch mixes.

Warp   http://members.tripod.com/~grantmcl/
The Spice Girls   warpspicegirls.html

Utterly, utterly brilliant. At last we all get to make a terrible mess of the wannabe sisters. Go carefully on sweet Baby Bunton's chin.

Information/Reference

Aardvarks Best of the Web http://www.stl-music.com/hub.html

Superb hub site providing links to the best composer, band, musician and event updates. Classical and pop both covered. Not all of the links work unfortunately.

Amazing Discographies   http://ad.techno.org

Like the man says, amazing discographies of every obscure, fly-by-night dance label you can think of, plus links to websites if they exist. Phew!

Bigmouth   http://www.bigmouth.co.uk
Billed as the UK's number-one music information station, it does
have remarkable amounts of everything you could possibly
imagine, from the more conventional news and tour dates to lists
of record labels and rehearsal rooms.

Great Singers   http://www.greatsingers.co.uk/index.html
Over 300 biographies of great singers and groups.

House Of Blues   http://www.hob.com
A huge magazine-style resource focusing on rock and rap music;
everything from news to video on artists ranging from Puff Daddy
to Twisted Sister, Cypress Hill to Supersuckers.

Insomniazine   http://www.insomniazine.co.uk
A London what's-on magazine. Full coverage of all the latest events
gives way to recommendations on the right bars, clubs, shops and
trousers. Good for live dates listings.

Music and Audio http://www.musicandaudio.com/artistal.shtml
User friendly guide to music on the web with links to masses of
artist pages plus a 'Great Myths of the Music Business' section.

Music Station   http://www.musicnewswire.com
Calling itself a global music information network, this site makes
obsessive lists of categorised and alphabetised news stories. There
are also Top Feature Stories and Top Review Stories. One for those
of a more retentive inclination, perhaps.

National Sound   http://www.bl.uk/collections
Archive   /sound-archive
The biggest sound archive in the world. Music lovers could wander
these dusty cyber-passages for years.

Rock Music Music Network   http://www.rock.com/
A guide and a store. Audio-stream tracks before you decide to buy.
More background detail on the artists than other online stores plus
MP3s.

Y2k-Music.Co.Uk   http://www.y2k-music.co.uk
New bands, artists and music of all kinds. Free audio samples, free
classified advertising and hassle-free CD shopping. Discover the
newest, freshest music online.

Jazz

All About Jazz   http://www.allaboutjazz.com
A 'Beginner's Guide to Jazz' and a database of popular jazz slang
words are two of the stand-outs on this massive site for jazz fans
which also offers reviews, interviews, listings and links.

Jazz Net   http://www.culturekiosque.com/jazz
Fairly highbrow features on contemporary and classic jazz music.

Jazz Online   http://www.jazzonln.com
Solid and no-nonsense site with everything you would expect:
artist biographies, new releases, CD sales, interviews, events, and
feature articles plus 'Jazz Messenger', an online jazz expert you can
email your questions to – 'No question too big or too small'.

Jazz Services   http://www.jazzservices.org.uk/jazzsite.htm
Charity funded by the Arts Council of England, providing
information, touring, education, publishing and communications.
Links to over 1,500 jazz and jazz-related websites.

New Jazz Archives   http://www.eyeneer.com/Jazz/index.html
A selective database of information on jazz artists.

Kitsch

Chas 'n' Dave　　　　http://www.chasndave.freeserve.co.uk
Everything you could possibly want to know about the Rabbit duo,
including a guide to cockney rhyming slang.

Collecting　　　　　　http://ourworld.compuserve.com/
Crap Records　　　　　homepages/plasterboard_towers
Fancy 'It's All Going Up Up Up' by Ronnie Corbett or 'I'm Backing
Britain' by Bruce Forsyth? No? OK, then, but this is a fascinatingly
compulsive collection of the worst music – and artwork – ever to
come under the misleading heading 'pop'.

Live Music

Aloud　　　　　　　　http://www.aloud.com/festival.shtml
A festivals page from the publishers of Select magazine and others.
It delivers a useful wodge of details, links and updates on
Glastonbury, Creamfields and All Tomorrow's Parties.

Glastonbury　　　　　http://www.glastonbury-festival.
Festival　　　　　　　co.uk/2000
Everything you have ever wanted to know about the festival's
history, the surrounding area, Pilton, or indeed the organiser,
Michael Eavis. Come here for the countdown to the year's event,
the dates, the spec, but no line-up details until May. You can also
find out about working there.

Lastminute.com　　　　http://www.lastminute.com
The much-talked-about UK resource is very good on live music with
ticket deals on London shows, plus great one-offs like the chance
to see 'the rock band of the 90s' in Paris in front of an invited
audience of only 1,000 people for only £249. It's Oasis, by the way.

Live Concerts   http:/liveconcerts.com
Possibly the best live-gig site, or guide portal, linking you with whatever gigs are currently online.

Pollstar   http://www.pollstar.com
A weekly updated source of worldwide gigs and concerts from the company that's been doing it in the real world for 20 years. The features and links are good too.

Rolling   http://www.rollingstone.tunes.com/
Stone   sections/localmusic
It's all here, city by US city. All the shows listed and updated weekly. Stay and read the rest of it, too. It's an education for absolutely nothing.

SFX.COM   http://www.sfx.com
SFX promotes live entertainment in all genres. Buy tickets for mainly US shows online.

Ticketmaster   http://www.ticketmaster.co.uk/
Tickets for the gig, buy or sell! Order online for individual shows or for UK festivals this year.

Lyrics

Lyrics World   http://www.lyricsworld.com
Currently the most useful search site on the web, which will find out whether there are any lyrics out there for the artist of your choice.

Songfile   http://www.lyrics.ch/index.htm
Punch in the words you half remember and hopefully this site will tell you the song and the artist. Doesn't always work. The service is part of http://www.songfile.com/, a site that also does sheet music and promises a large online store very soon.

Original Hip Hop Lyrics Archive   **http://www.ohhla.com**
Check out this site for a definitive archive of the best of rap words; find out just what Li'l Kim was going on about, discover the truth behind claims of violence-glamorisation and lewdness.

The Home Of Television   **http://www.geocities.com/**
Theme Lyrics   **Hollywood/Academy/4760**
Thanks to this very strange enthusiast, you can name the show – whether it's 60s, 70s, 80s or 90s – and check out the theme to your fave comedy, action series, or romantic drama. So come on – they're altogether cookie ...

Big Index   **http://www.myths.com/pub/lyrics/bigindex.html**
The author of this site confesses right at the start that it is made up purely of songs he likes, but the list is long and impressive – the Clash to the Beatles to loads of one-hit wonders.

Miscellaneous: Merchandise, Campaigns

Campaign For   **http://www.eff.**
Audiovisual Free Expression   **org/cafe**
Piracy of an artist's work is illegal. Fair use is not. A worthwhile campaign.

First Look   **http://www.firstlook.com**
Not an MP3 site, but similar in style, it gives a chart of established and newer artists all keen to promote their records. You can listen to snippets, then decide whether you want to buy. Often tracks are posted here before general release.

Nervous Records   **http://www.nervousnyc.com**
New York's hip dance label, home to Byron Stingly, Josh Wink and that distinctive cartoon logo. The merchandise page is worth the price of admission alone.

Road Recovery http://www.roadrecovery.com/clear.gif

A worthy cause for musicians who may have indulged a little too much. Worth visiting if only for the heroin-chic T-shirts marked 'Sex will no longer interest you, but stealing might'.

War Child http://www.warchild.org

The ongoing campaign to help innocent victims of war, this charity counts Eno, Bowie and Pavarotti as patrons.

Wilson And Allroys Record Reviews http://www.warr.org

'We listen to the lousy records so you won't have to!' Absolutely fantastic, self-deprecating, informed and witty reviews of over 2,000 records.

Music Industry

For more industry resources, have a look in Chapter 9.

Applause http://www.cnvi.com/applause

Tips on getting into the business, mammoth lists of advice and links. Hooray!

Bip http://www.bipbipbip.com

A place for independent musicians to sell music directly to the public.

Fact 42 Online http://www.fact42.com

'May there always be a cold beer with you,' they say. News, job opps and other fascinating stuff from the concert touring industry.

Roadie Net http://roadie.net

Sob stories, job opps, tales of large riders and why all artists are bastards. This is the site for anyone who has ever humped someone else's gear. Great pictures too.

Miow   http://www.miow.com
London based MP3 site with industry tips, links and chat.

Net4Music   http://www.net4music.com
Based in France, this is an artist-friendly webzine with a massive catalogue of digital scores and MIDI files, sheet music, chords, lyrics, articles and star interviews, all geared towards the working musician.

Opera

Eon   http://www.european-opera-network.org/en
The European Opera Network is dedicated to expanding communication and co-operation among opera companies across Europe and around the world in partnership with OPERA America.

Operabase   http://www.operabase.com
Search using singer, conductor, producer, even character, via the online database. Plus listings from around the world with excellent contact details of individual theatres plus synopses, biographies and libretti.

Royal Opera House   http://www.royalopera.org
Information, pictures and booking for the opera fan living in or visiting London.

Photography

Great Modern Pictures   http://greatmodernpictures.com
John Lennon, David Bowie, the Sex Pistols, Iggy – a New York Gallery online with a substantial archive of Bob Gruen, Mick Rock and other seminal rock photographers' work. The scans could be better, but you can buy online and own a classic limited print. Award-winning.

Steve Double   http://www.double-whammy.com
A site predominantly for the biz, but worth checking out for
fantastic shots of most relevant artists of the last ten years, from Air
to Wu-Tang Clan. The scan quality is superb too.

Rock Around The World   http://www.ratw.com
US mag from the 70s with a good photo library and links to its radio
show archive.

Waring Abbott   http://www.waringabbott.com
Famous for Kiss photographs, this company has pictures from
every genre, Lou Reed to jazz to Rod Stewart.

Punk/New Wave

G.G. Allin   http://www.chebucto.ns.ca/~ac139/ggallin
A great site detailing just how relentlessly offensive and nasty this
little-known, sociopathic, scatological, but highly influential US
hardcore punk rocker was before he did the decent thing and
overdosed.

Punk Rock In Brighton   http://whodeenyproductions.com/punk
Well-written and -illustrated trawl through the history of largely
anonymous but always hilarious bands from the south coast of
the UK.

Punk Rock Women   http://www.comnet.ca/~rina/index.html
Really definitive: from the Adverts to X-Ray Spex.

Trouser Press   http://www.trouserpress.com
The legendary anglophile US rock magazine has put all its back
issues on line. Search for the most obscure old punk band and get
a brilliantly written history and full discography.

Radio

Bring The Noise!   http://bringthenoise.com
'The corporations have failed to globalize the genre at its best. We
at Bringthenoise do that'. New and exclusive hip-hop web-radio
broadcasts from the irrepressible Chuck D.

Broadcast Music   http://www.broadcastmusic.com
'Where the world comes to listen', they claim, but it's hard to
disagree as they are one of the largest web broadcasting
companies in the world, offering syndicated as well as exclusive live
radio broadcasts of all music genres, alternative, blues, classical,
jazz, country and Top 40.

Choice Radio   http://www.choiceradio.com
CMJ's website of the week, this site is one of the best Internet radio
channels with a clear map of the genre channels (rock to classical
to Latin) on the homepage, and an opportunity to vote on tracks
and really get involved. Once you have registered it's a joy.

GLR   http://www.bbc.co.uk/england/glr
London's best radio station offers an excellent community site with
each show having its own page: godlike Gideon Coe transcribes
the excellent 'Soundtrack of Our Lives', a countdown of listeners'
favourite music of all time, and Charlie Gillett recommends music
we might never have heard without him.

Nordic   http://www.nordicdms.com/radio/site/NEW
Online radio, plus an MP3 archive with free audio players, a vinyl
database, links and web rings. Even a T-shirt gallery.

Radio 1   http://www.bbc.co.uk/radio1
This is fab. From Whitney Houston to Basement Jaxx, from Snuff to
Travis. With a studio-cam, Real Player audio streams, and a guide to

brand-new music courtesy of The Evening Session, it's a great way to start getting used to music online.

Radio 2   **http://www.bbc.co.uk/radio2**

No longer the butt of jokes, this BBC radio station has transformed itself into the station for jazz, folk, country, new country and rock 'n' roll fans with credible DJs like Mark Lamarr, Jonathan Ross and Paul Gambaccini. The site unfortunately still seems a little stuck in the 80s.

Radio 3   **http://www.bbc.co.uk/radio3**

An excellent classical station which also deals in post-rock and experimental music. You can listen to music online via Real Audio and they also have a database of the best classical recordings, which you can use to search for music you may have chanced upon while tuning in.

Record Producers

Any of you in need of a producer will find a more than helpful section in Chapter 9. What follows is a selection of some of the more interesting sites dedicated to the world's most renowned helmsmen. And a couple of directories to help you on your way. Prepare to be disappointed, though, as many producers – even some of the bigger names – have not yet got around to building sites. Probably expecting an engineer to do it for them ...

A Dictionary of   **http://www.officialsmithereens.com/**
Record Producers   **dikenwriting.html**

The dictionary itself is, sadly, not yet online (well, not as I write this, anyway). But you can find helpful excerpts here.

The Dust Brothers   **http://www.dustbrothers.com**

Load up with Flash and get down with the guys who produced the

Beastie Boys, Beck and ... Tone Loc. The site is as cool as they are. Check out the Dustography.

Brian Eno   http://www.hyperreal.org/music/artists/brian_eno
Enoweb contains everything you could possibly want to know about the visionary artist and producer (U2, James, Bowie, Talking Heads etc.) There's an 'Ask Eno' section, a full biography and discography, plus a selection of photos of his installations.

John Leckie   http://www.mill.net/dumyhead/leckielinks.html
The man who produced the Stone Roses and Radiohead.

William Orbit   http://www.williamorbit.com
Worth visiting, even if you are not a fan of the current Madonna and Blur producer, simply because this site is an example of beautiful graphics, lovingly compiled listings, and all-round sonic and visual perfection. Fascinating.

Lee 'Scratch'   http://homepage.oanet.com/
Perry   sleeper/scratch.htm
On The Wire is a brilliant tribute to the bonkers king of ska, reggae and dub. We are greeted with the words 'This Is Upsetting' and are then offered a pleasing and extensive choice of scratch stuff. Also worth skanking to is the Perry madness at http://www.furious.com/perfect/leeperry, which is brimful of attitude.

Studiobase Record   http://www.demon.co.uk/
Producers List A-Z   studiobase/producer
A little UK-centric, but very handy if you want to find out who it was who mixed the life out of those Supergrass tracks you thought were kickin' live.

Tony Visconti   http://www.tonyvisconti.com/
A really well-put-together page from the Bolan, Bowie and Seahorses producer.

Reggae

About Ska/Reggae   http://ska.about.com
Once again those About people score highly on the information-
gathering front. This is one of their most thoroughly researched
pages and links to everything reggae- or ska-related, from early
Mento to the Two Tone Revival, to the so-called New Ska
Movement, big in California.

Discover   http://discoverjamaica.com/
Kingston   gleaner/discover/kingston.html
Everything about the reggae capital of the world: historical
information, maps, enticing photography and the opening times of
the Bob Marley Museum.

Heartbeat Records   http://www.rounder.com/heartbeat
The best reggae/ska reissue label with over 200 original Jamaican
titles. Its catalogue includes many from Clement 'Coxone' Dodd's
Studio One label featuring artists such as Lee Perry, the Skatellites,
the Ethiopians and early Bob Marley.

The Real Jamaica Ska   http://www.slip.not/~skajam
Not updated enough, but then Jamaican ska music is a 60s
phenomenon anyway. This is a decent resource featuring a potted
history, Prince Buster pictures and much more offbeat fun.

Reggae Lyrics Archive   http://hem.passagen.se/selahis
Quite a lot about Jah and his children.

Reggae Ring   http://www.reggaering.org
Jah bless this hub site, which links to all the locations you need.

Reggae Sunsplash   http://www.reggaesunsplash.com
Info about the fabulous annual festival.

Reggae Train   **http://www.reggaetrain.com**
Comprehensive and organised, this is one of the finest websites in the crowded genre of reggae. It boasts a good artist database, online radio and seems to update its news frequently.

Reggae Web   **http://www.reggaeweb.com/main.htm**
An excellent news source.

Ruff Cut   **http://www.ruffkut.com**
Hear streamed audio of original reggae mixes.

Shm Records   **http://www.shmrecords.com**
Used vinyl. If you are into the original ska and reggae releases from 1960 to 1985, then come and blow your readies here.

Skinheads – The Good,   **http://www.macropolis.**
The Bad and The Ugly   **demon.co.uk**
A history of the skinhead movement, focusing on the importance of Jamaican music. The snippets of violent imagery from Stanley Kubrick's *A Clockwork Orange* are a tad worrying, though.

R&B/Modern Soul

88HipHop   **http://www.88hiphop.com**
A brilliant and stuffed New York zine which offers news, links, webcasts ... oh, you name it. A must for hip-hop fans, so bookmark the mother.

The Booty Bone   **http://www.freeserve.com**
Formally the Mothership Connection, this funk primer deals with the thorny issues of exactly what 'The Funk' is, where it's at, and who is currently responsible for it.

CJ's House of Soul   **http://www.flavourtown.com**
CJ's house maintains that it is 'Vibin' at all times'. Not bad, but could do with a bit more updating.

Ejams   http://www.ejams.com

They claim to be 'Keepin' it Real For Ya!' and who can possibly argue with that when they are offering piles of free downloads and plenty of chat rooms?

The R&B Page   http://www.rbpage.com

Reliable resource if you like sexy modern soul and R&B. From swing beat to two-step garage. Up-to-date coverage leaning towards the traditional rather than the ground-breaking; artists featured are the likes of Chaka Khan and Natalie Cole.

Rhythm and Blues Music Primer   http://www.the primer.org

Focusing on the days when R&B meant Wilson Pickett, Sam and Dave, and Booker T and the MGs, this site smokes like Steve Cropper's fingers.

StreetSounds from Pseudo   http://www.ssound.pseudo.com

A homepage from New York, this offers up-to-date R&B news, interviews with artists such as Giles Peterson, plus links to a weekly radio broadcast called 88-Soul, which promises all the up-and-coming R&B talent, and subsite, http://www.koolout.com, which specialises in Real Video footage.

Vibe   http://www.vibe.com/main

Quincy Jones established this guide to R&B, hip-hop, soul and reggae and it's a decently written and fairly informative magazine – read the reviews and hear audio samples.

Whoopass   http://www.btinternet.com/~labid.malik

Contemporary R&B, hip-hop and soul, deep from the heart of the United Kingdom of Great Britain. Or something.

Sampling

Samplenet   http://www.samplenet.co.uk
A great resource of sampling information, including a database of
thousands of free samples and info on hardware etc.

Hollywood Edge http://www.hollywoodedge.com/samples.html
Part of a much larger resource, this page is the place to go for
that deep lion's roar you absolutely must have for the end of the
track.

Soundtracks

Austin Powers   http://www.maverickrc.com/
Soundtrack   austinpowers
Brilliant for soundtrack lovers, including Real Audio clips of all the
best tracks and requisite Dr Evil screensavers.

John   http://www.geosites.com/hollywood/
Barry   bungalow2/barry/jbarry.htm
A good fan site with exhaustive documentation on the current
activities and past glories of the greatest film-score composer ever.

Dress Circle   http://www.dresscircle.co.uk
Specialises in both film soundtracks and music from theatre
productions. The very best of Broadway and beyond, with some
RealAudio previews in case you can't quite choose between South
Pacific and Seven Brides for Seven Brothers. If you can't say no, get
them both.

Film Music.Com   http://www.filmmusic.com
Host to the superb Cinemusic.net music resource, this also has a
very useful database.

Film Music Magazine   http://filmmusicmag.com

Intended for the industry and therefore certainly one to bookmark for film-score fans, it offers links film-music-related locations.

Soundtrack Auction   http://www.cisf.com/auction/index.shtml

An auction for soundtracks – just sign up and start bidding for thousands of categories of vintage records. Delicious, if a little expensive.

Soundtrack Net   http://www.soundtrack.net

More useful for new soundtrack recordings than for vintage ones, but packed with useful release details and features, plus links to five other search engines.

Sheet Music

Boosey And Hawkes   http://www.boosey.coml

International classical music publishers – and instrument shop – offers a content-rich site.

Sheet Music Plus   http://www.sheetmusicplus.com

Fast-search for sheet music in the way you would at an online CD store.

Songbooks

Guitar Tab Archives   http://www.cc.umist.ac.uk

Right, so the bottom E-string is dropped to a D in 'Dear Prudence'. No wonder we were having trouble. Everything from classic rock to reggae to indie.

The Who   http://www.thewho.net/whotabs

Loads of Who tunes for the guitar, some of them quite easy to play.

Soul

The Primer http://www.theprimer.org.uk
Get all the features, record tips and more in your email inbox if you subscribe to this meticulous and good-looking site.

Soul A Go-Go http://www.soul-a-go-go.demon.co.uk
A virtual jukebox packed with obscure Northern Soul classics such as Sammy Davis Jnr doing a vocal version of the Hawaii 5-0 theme. Brilliant.

Soul On The Net http://www.personal.cet.ac.il/yonin
Lovingly compiled by Yoni – audio streams, pictures and articles covering the period when Soul meant just that, plus a Reggae Got Soul link.

The Stax Site http://perso.wanadoo.fr/stax.site
Catch up on the latest news, sadly much of which is obituaries owing to the age of this Memphis label, who brought us Sam and Dave, Otis Redding, Booker T and the MGs and many more.

Sweden

We've all grooved to the Cardigans, the Wannadies, Whale and Andreas Johnson, not to mention Salt, Drain and the exceptional Souls. From pop to rock, indie to metal, Sweden is happening and no mistake. Peruse the following, and be first on the bandwagon.

Jimmy Fun Music http://www.jimmyfun.se
For a long time the future of pop has been Swedish, and this publisher goes a long way to prove just that. New artists are audio streamed, and current artists play us fresh material.

Soap   http://www.cabal.se/mnw/soap

The Wannadies' original label has a strong tradition of great power pop. Beautiful visuals produced in Scandinavian style.

TV and Video

Like Television   http://www.liketelevision.com/musicv

Offering something they call, with no hint of irony, 'Instant Gratification Streaming', this resource is pretty smart in its musical choices with programmes featuring Cream's farewell concert and a Duke Ellington show.

Live On The Net   http://www.liveonthenet.com

Aside from all the other items, such as sport and religion, this webcast hub station has a lot of music handily categorised by genre from classical through blues to Latino.

VH1   http://VH1.com

With downloads from Iggy Pop, collector auctions, the latest news and a 'Before They Were Stars' feature, this is not quite as good as the TV channel yet, but it really is getting there.

Virtue TV   http://www.virtuetv.com/music

Sail past all the other movie and fashion content and go directly to all your favourite turns on video – many of the shows like Suede or Supergrass are done in conjunction with the NAME. There are also video interviews with the likes of Mel C.

Weddings

Wedding Chappel   http://www.music.com/weddingchapel

Music.com's wedding service offers you general music tips for your wedding from Bach's 'Air on a G String' to Bryan Adams's 'Everything I Do'. While on the subject, did you hear about the bride who asked the band to play the Robin Hood theme while she was walking down the aisle? As she swept towards the altar, they burst into 'Robin Hood, Robin Hood, riding through the glen ...'

World Music

Ancient Future   http://www.ancient-future.com/index.html
Acclaimed site from this world music band who fuse an unusual blend of musical traditions from around the world. Packed with links.

BBC World Service   http://www.bbc.co.uk/worldservice/pop
The DJs Andy Kershaw and John Peel helm the flagship shows featured in this guide to the station's excellent coverage of new and unusual music.

Charlie Gillett   http://www.roughguides.com/charlie
Gillett, author of *Sound of the City* (one of the definitive works of music journalism), presents a homepage courtesy of Rough Guides, packed with erudite reviews of quality new and vintage artists.

Groovesite   http://www.groovesite.com
World music web-radio station with personality and charm.

Womad   http://womadusa.org
US-based page for the worldwide organisation, stuffed full of events, news and artist features.

World Music Charts http://www.weltmusik.de/charts/main.htm
Since 1997, 40 journalists have been compiling these weekly charts from Africa and beyond.

World Music Homepage   http://w3.to/worldmusic
So many links, such a big planet.

9//WE WANT IT ALL, WE WANT IT ALL ...

Despite hopes to the contrary in venues, rehearsal rooms and demo studios all over the world, the Internet does not allow new artists to get away without the usual requisites – hard work and being talented. There is still no substitute for originality and good tunes. However if you have It – that certain special *je ne sais quoi* – as we're sure you do if you're reading this, then the Internet is one extra tool to be used in conjunction with Jiffy bags, cold-calls and banging on doors. The most common, almost *de rigueur*, choice for new artists is the self-designed homepage.

In every homepage a heartache
Your chief consideration before you start worrying about what sort of font you're going to have, is whether, in fact, having a website is going to help your band at all. What are your reasons for having one? How are people going to hear about the site? And are you going to deliver them something worthwhile when they get there? It's all very well being great live, but if potential fans arrive at your page only to discover a stock animated gif (one of those moving graphics that are neither functional nor pleasing to the eye) and a misspelled lyric sheet, your cover may be blown.

Most musicians who have made their own homepage have various pet do's and don'ts, which – reminiscent of the time you asked for advice on purchasing a computer – are wildly contradictory, depending on whom you ask. That said, there are four basic steps:

1   **Get a host for your homepage.** The cheapest way to do this is to go to your ISP, which will often offer you free

webspace as part of their package. The downside of this
is that it usually won't be that much space, probably
between 10 and 50 megabytes.

If you want to have any animated gifs or MP3s, it's better
to go a host that can offer you enough megabytes to do all
this: type in 'site hosting' in your search engine, or go to
Host Index at http://www.hostindex.com. One good US
host is Pair Networks on http://pair.com who charge
roughly $10 a month.

2   **Get a domain name**. The key to this is registering a URL
    (Internet address) as close to your band name as possible –
    it's no good giving out an address that no one will
    remember. Often you can get this sorted out at the same
    time as you get your host, most of whom will register the
    name for you.

    Registering your own domain name is also inexpensive and
    simple: try UK2. Net at http://uk2net.co.uk or Easily on
    http://www.easily.co.uk. If you do register your name
    separately you may need to enlist the help of a trusty,
    technologically minded mate who will link up your name
    with the host's server. Just remember, if your band is called
    Yahoo, it may be time for a name change.

3   **Design it**. If you want total control over the layout and
    look of your pages – which, if you are a true artist, we are
    betting you do – it is worth getting to know the basics of
    HTML, the language used to construct web pages. It is not
    hard to learn and there are several websites out there that
    give you the basics of web design. A basic introductory one
    is Jonny's HTML Headquarters at http://webhelp.org or

HTML For The Rest Of Us at **http://www.geocities.com/SiliconValley/Lakes/3933/frame.htm**.

If you really can't be bothered, then your browser is a good place to start to find software packages designed to make homepage construction as easy as writing your band's logo on a toilet door: if you have Internet Explorer it's called Front Page Express; if you have Netscape Navigator, it's Composer.

When designing your band's homepage it's important to think about aesthetics: legible text, good picture scans, pages laid out to minimise awkward scrolling and so on. It is also a good idea to imagine the length of time potential fans, who may have liked your tape, record or gig, and now want to access your site, will devote to waiting for it to download. There is no point in designing an amazing Shockwave graphic of yourself windmilling your guitar, if most of your potential fans don't have the software or the patience for it to load.

Tips on web design can be found on **http://www.highfive.com** but it's a good idea to look at the sites of bands that you like – bearing in mind that artists like Beck and Radiohead have a little more money to play with than you.

While looking, you can see how they were created very easily by clicking on View, then Source, if you are in Internet Explorer, or Page Source if you are in Netscape Navigator. The code the pages are written in will miraculously appear, and you will get a better idea of how they did it. Better still is looking at some of the many terrible sites, none of which, we are proud to say, are in this book. Mistakes are obvious things like, for example, assuming everyone finds you fascinating: who wants to read a long list of influences, equipment, or lyrics for a band they may have only a casual interest in? Give them quality pictures, upcoming gigs and interesting stuff that's particular to you. As with the letter you send out to record companies with your demo, keep your site full of attitude, wit and personality.

4 **Just add music.** Putting your own music on your homepage is the next logical step and it is quite simple. To get MP3s uploaded you first need to transfer or 'rip off' your recordings to a AIFF or WAV (pronounced wave) file. This is an uncompressed music file which takes up a large amount of space – around 40Mb per track – on the hard drive. If you put the CD into your computer's ROM drive, it will appear 'mounted' on your desktop if you have a Mac, or the CD-ROM symbol will appear if you are using Windows for PC. To convert each track to an AIFF or WAV file, you need to use a program such as Audio Catalyst.

A useful resource for finding this is MP3.Com's help page on **http://help.mp3.com/help/faqs/setup.html**. Once in WAV form, the track must be converted into MP3 format with an encoder programme. There are many of these available to download free from the web. Try Shareware at **http://www.shareware.com**, or search for 'MP3 encoder' in your search field. Once you have this, your tracks can be reduced to a mere 4Mb, a tenth of their original size – and you can delete all the original WAV files that are taking up all that space of your hard disk.

Now comes the fun part – uploading on to your website. To do this, you need something called FTP (File Transfer Protocol), which enables you to connect to your website structure. This structure is made up of HTML code, graphics and anything else you may have put on your site, so you can't simply send it files or messages by email and expect it to understand them. Hence FTP. Get an FTP client such as Cute FTP (**http://www.cuteftp.com**) or Get Right (**http://www.getright.com**) and follow their simple instructions.

Once your tracks are up there, simply add an html link for each of your files to connect them to your site. Fans and casual visitors will then see a 'download MP3' graphic for each of your songs, and will be able to download with a mere click. Alternatively – they should also be able to stream your music. Just make sure it IS all your own music, though!

What your site can do for you
Your website is also a brilliant way of building a database of fans which you can galvanise into action whenever you need to. No more standing outside the pub, handing out flyers, or, worse still, paying for postage. Once you have collected enough of a database you can send everyone news of your forthcoming gig/release in a single email. A note of warning, though: don't expect that emailing industry types you don't know will win you any favours. They will resent the impertinence and you will risk your work not being taken seriously.

Do remember to take advantage of the traffic going both ways. Your fan base can communicate with you from all over the world via your homepage's email address, letting you know how much they enjoyed your MP3 tracks and asking you impatiently when they can hear some new stuff. Many struggling musicians find that occasional positive email feedback from just a handful of enthusiastic listeners is enough to sustain them through years of rejection and negativity. A little praise goes a long way. Do take this praise for what it's worth though. You may have 200 adulatory emails from all over the planet, but this just means that you could be popular everywhere, not that you are. Having 200 rabid fans would secure you a gig at many venues, but not if they're in 200 different towns on five separate continents.

If you have some spare cash and no time in between writing songs, you could pay someone to design a homepage for you. Increasingly there seem to be friends of friends who are prepared to 'do you a great site for five hundred quid'. Check the credentials of these people thoroughly though: even generic webspace packages like Netscape charge thousands more than this, and, despite these people peppering their pitch with words like 'Dreamweaver' and 'Javascript', they may only know marginally more than you do. The chances are, you could do the same thing better yourself. It's better if you do, as all sites are more impressive when they're continually updated. People – fans, peers and site controllers – tend to take you more seriously. It shows that you care, that you make things happen (to some, the very essence of rock 'n' roll). Put in the effort – it will serve you well.

MP3: Digit-lickin' good
People who can possibly really help your career in pop are the Unsigned Band MP3 Sites which are springing up at an increasing rate. Getting your tracks on most of them is not a problem, but deciding on the ones that will work for you is.

The key thing to bear in mind is how much traffic an MP3 site gets.

Bands who use these sites recommend 'working' them to maximise their effect. Don't get your page posted, then sit back expecting to be REM. For example, if the site has a chart, get in it, because human nature dictates that this will be self-perpetuating: if someone sees something is number 1 or even number 9, they'll be much more inclined to listen to it. You can do this by 'working' the bulletin boards – getting yourself mentioned a lot, and also putting the URL segued into your page on all your flyers and posters. And if the site starts getting loads of traffic to your page then they will start doing you favours. Also, add a link to your homepage if you have one. That way you can direct more traffic to your site, where you offer the promise of exclusive MP3s, pictures and so on.

Working the MP3 sites: a few extra tips
A few other tips. Spend time perusing and adding to the bulletin boards, and make your presence felt in any chat rooms going. Make friends. This is an indie community and consequently self-supporting, but it will support you only if it knows who you are. Once you've made friends with members of other bands who are also plugging their music and pages, link up (if you think what they do is good, mind). That way you'll get some of their traffic too. Who knows, you might even end up sharing a bill at Wembley Stadium, or at least in your hometowns? Pool your live audiences – you'll stand a much better chance of getting gigs if you can guarantee the promoter a reasonable attendance. Some UK indie bands, with no deal at all, have used connections made on MP3 sites to play as far afield as Paris and New York. Go student, organise a working exchange trip – but do your best to ensure your

new MP3 buddies can be trusted. You don't want to end up at JFK Airport with all your gear and nowhere to stay.

It's worth considering your own musical influences, and making a list of acts whose fans might also like your music. Contact their official sites and sites put up by their greatest fans. Explain your humble devotion to the cause. See if you can't get your site linked to theirs. Imagine the traffic if you got hooked up with Slipknot, or Dream Theater or – gulp! – REM.

Getting famous can cost you dearly
The Godfather of all MP3 sites is MP3.com (http://www.mp3.com), which remains a favourite among unsigned bands. As well as this, the amount of traffic this site gets is way ahead of any of the competition. They make no claim on the copyright of your material, and they split any profits from sales of CDs with you 50/50 (they 'burn' and post out the CDs themselves). Also, despite MP3 downloads being free to the public, they will pay you for these as well. Cheers! The downside of this, and of many of the other MP3 sites mentioned below, is that there is no quality control – complete equality in fact – resulting in a mammoth list of genres from ambient through country to techno. If you click on alternative, for example, you get reams of Californian straight-edge bands, who, while all being very competent, are remarkably similar-sounding.

Think hard before you part with any of the folding stuff. Many sites will put up your music for nothing, taking payment only for CD sales and paid-for downloads. Others, though, charge quite extraordinary amounts for their services. The Orchard, for instance, charges $40 for administration, $50 for sound clips, $15 for a biography, $10 for links, $7 each for press quotes and tour dates and $5 for additional photos. Soon adds up, doesn't it? Other sites demand set-up fees of around $35, still more ask for between five and 20 CDs. Some will add your name to their mailed-out indie catalogue for a further $25 a month. These people do help to further your cause but, even if you work the MP3 sites hard, you'll probably still only have sales of somewhere in the low hundreds. With each CD sold at maybe $6 each, and 50 per cent being taken by the sites, you really don't want to be spending too much on promotion.

Newer sites such as the heavily advertised Peoplesound (http://www.peoplesound.com), boast a hands-on A&R involvement: you will get posted on the site only if the team like your music. This, in theory, promotes an image of inherent quality and encourages fans to return and be adventurous, sampling unknowns like you. Arriving at Peoplesound, music fans are given a field in which they can type in the sort of music they like by artist or genre – for instance, Curtis Mayfield or hard rock. This prompts the genre-activated database and immediately offers a list of artists who may just be the sort of thing they like. The job for you as an artist, is to categorise yourself realistically and honestly on the application form – no use saying you sound like the Verve when you are edging towards Gary Barlow.

Something old, something new

The question does remain though: who is listening to your music in this way? The 'revolution' that the web promises for new music is a terrifying leveller: everyone becomes equal – equally successful, equally anonymous. And the best stuff may remain obscured behind teetering piles of rubbish. Unless of course, artists think laterally and combine the new technology with more traditional marketing normally associated with the old guard – the record companies.

The US country band Roger Clyne and the Peacemakers did just that. By working their host site, and by emblazoning its logo and URL on all their T-shirts and flyers, they garnered attention way beyond the minuscule 1,200 downloads their music received, and made number one in the Billboard Internet Album Sales Chart.

Meanwhile in the UK, the indie band Stumble got themselves accepted by Peoplesound, then went one further: they employed a PR person and a plugger. The result? Plays on Radio 1 and XFM, reviews in NME and Kerrrang! and consequent interest from major labels. And all this from a song called 'How Many Times Do I Have to Kill You Before You Die?'.

Inevitably, major labels are now coming round to the idea that the web can be useful in discovering new talent. In the US, Universal have recently started Jimmy and Doug's Farm Club (http://farmclub.com), where you can, in theory at least, get your material listened to by the one-time U2 producer Jimmy Iovine and possibly end up with a record deal.

There are many companies, some of the better ones in the Address Book below, offering similar utopias, claiming to be able to hook you up with the major label of your dreams. Get Signed (http://www.getsigned.com), which has lengthy interviews with successful A&R personal, and A&R Online (http://www.aandronline.com) both make similar bold claims. There are others which charge you for their services such as the UK's A&R Bandit (http://www.wightweb.demon.co.uk/bandit) and the USA's Taxi (http://www.taxi.com). The latter offers a tempting but expensive link-up service with a massive network of experienced music-business executives who could take your demo to the right A&R person in a suitable company.

So go on, what are you waiting for? Network on the Net! But get your hands dirty as well: use the web for all the traditional things you're going to need like equipment, a manager, a lawyer. Right now it offers a fairly comprehensive directory of all the possible resources you may need, from CD manufacturers to songwriting forums. Remember, though, that, just because a company has a URL, it doesn't automatically make it the best: it just means it has more time on its hands, which isn't necessarily a good thing. There are, despite this, loads of sites that for years the industry has been crying out for: try the Band Register (**http://www. bandreg.com**) to make sure no one has already claimed your band name; get advice from the Musicians' Union (**http://www. musiciansunion.org.uk**), hopefully without being left listening to their hold music; or try to come up with better rhymes than Noel Gallagher with the Online Rhyming Dictionary (**http://www. link.cs.cmu.edu/dougb/rhyme-doc.html**), or maybe with the help of your three-year-old sister.

With all these resources available at the click of a mouse, it's hard to believe that if you are in any way talented you could fall through the, er ... net.

//ADDRESS BOOK

A&R Virtually

Many musicians like to think that the Internet will allow them to break big without selling their souls to the record companies. It's a naïve and foolish notion – after all, while you're struggling away

*trying to build a fan base, doesn't it make more sense to be
spending someone else's money? Here's where to find it.*

A&R Online   http://www.aandronline.com
Get a record deal.

Bandit A&R   http://www.wightweb.demon.co.uk/
Newsletter   bandit
UK monthly version of TAXI. A three-issue subscription is cheaper at
£15 or $25, and a list of satisfied customers says something.

Band Utopia 2000   http://www.bandutopia.com
Global help given for bands. Great links.

Become A Rock Star   http://www.tt.net/ultramodern/vinnie
Ten Amusing Commandments To Rock Star wannabes.

Billboard Talent Net   http://www.billboardtalentnet.com
An enhanced, 24-hour, global interactive link to the world of new
and emerging musical artists. Right.

Get Signed   http://www.getsigned.com
Exclusive in-depth interviews with industry insiders plus loads of
handy hints on getting that elusive deal and the mistakes you
should avoid making.

Jimmy And Doug's Farm   http://farmclub.com
Two senior Universal executives, Jimmy Iovine (of U2 fame)
and Doug Morris, have started up this site – like a major-label
Peoplesound – for unsigned bands. A farm club usually means a
baseball training camp – here, bands are encouraged to send in
material on MP3 format, which will be listened to by experienced
A&R types, then, if given the thumbs-up, posted on the site.

Music Unsigned   http://www.musicunsigned.com
It's about knowing the game, as they say.

Never Off Key   http://www.neveroffkey.com
Advice at a price.

Remote Music   http://www.remotemusic.com
Get 'The Millennium Prayer' for 99p. Their mission, which they have chosen to accept, is to become one of the world's first true online record companies. With Cliff Richard and Babylon Zoo.

Stargig   http://www.stargig.com
Promises to be an alternative to traditional record companies run by the man who founded Chrysalis Records, Terry Ellis.

Taxi   http://www.taxi.com
Much-touted US independent A&R site which connects unsigned artists and songwriters to new-act-hungry record labels and publishers via its own team of veteran industry A&R figures. The list of A&R personnel is impressive as, indeed, it should be for the annual subscription of $299.95, plus a $5-per-tape/CD submission fee.

Annual Events

For those of you willing to travel far for success, here are a few of the bigger industry get-togethers. Why not find out when they are, involve yourself, hand out some flyers and CDs? You really could do yourself a big favour.

CMJ   http://www.cmj.com
New York in the summertime, with every A&R man, distributor, manufacturer, press officer, record company executive and top-line journalist you could ever possibly need. Maybe you should show your face, too.

In The City   http://www.inthecity.co.uk
Best new-music festival in Europe – get on a stage in front of the industry.

Midem   **http://www.midem.com**

The annual music business conference where you flog your
finished CDs.

Band Business

*The Internet doesn't just make it easier to reach your public,
it also offers a welter of sober advice. And plenty of inside jokes
too. If you think you're the only one who's suffered at the hands
of the industry, or if you're just not sure what's going on, read
on ...*

Band-O-Matic!   **http://www.joescafe.com/bands**

Need ideas for a band name? Go to this site. Need a good laugh in
your lunch hour? Ditto.

The Band Register   **http://www.bandreg.com**

Music industry-approved register of all the band names in the UK,
with details of when and where the bands were formed –
invaluable for artists and record companies alike.

British Unsigned Rock Bands   **http://www.burbs.org.uk**

A.k.a. Burbs, a free resource for bands to use and for the rest of the
world to enjoy, it has over 500 artists waiting to heard.

College Music   **http://www1.collegemusic.com**

US alternative rock tips.

Harmony Central   **http://www.harmonycentral.com**

A complete resource for musicians, from songwriting to contracts.
Brilliant.

Indie Biz.Com   **http://www.kathoderaymusic.com/indiebiz**

Gives industry networking a new meaning.

Indie Music http://www.indie-music.com

General music info for the US indie artist – links, record labels and bands.

Music Media http://www.music-media.co.uk

Lists of hundreds of UK bands looking for management, guitarists looking for drummers, drummers looking for bass players and bass players looking for the plot. No time-wasters.

Musicians Web http://www.musiciansweb.net

Showcase your material, plus resource links for musicians and songwriters.

Recording Hints For http://www.wserv.com/
The Poor ~dkennedy/page1.html

Useful before the advances start pouring in.

Studiobase http://www.demon.co.uk/studiobase

Expanding database of UK recording studios, record companies, rehearsal facilities, record producers etc.

Equipment

Whether you're a house-rockin' DJ looking for some wheels of steel, or a mad axeman seeking a guitar as cool as Jimmy Page's, you're in luck. As commerce expands across the web, music has not been left behind, and you can now use the Internet to find almost any hardware or software you might require. Happy hunting.

Digi Bid http://www.digibid.com

Online auction of new and used pro gear. A great money saver.

Etcetera http://www.etcetera.co.uk

PC software for musicians, plus a free demo disc. Time to get contemporary.

Evolution http://www.evolution.co.uk
UK keyboard controller manufacturer. Really good value.

Fender http://www.fender.com
Classic Strats and Telecasters. A slice of guitar heaven for all Ritchie Blackmore wannabes. We all went down to Montreux ...

Gearsearch http://www.gearsearch.com
Resource for finding instrument and equipment retailers. Excellent for beginners, and those spreading their wings.

Gibson Guitars http://www.gibson.com
Loads of beautiful things plus the magazine Amplifier on http://www.gibson.com/magazines/amplifier.

Guitar.Com http://www.guitar.com
Everything the best real-world guitar magazines offer, such as reviews, news and tests, plus the virtual bonus of MP3s and a forum.

Midifarm http://midifarm.com
One-stop destination for Midi files and other musicianly PC downloads. Come on, you gotta keep up!

Norwalk Music http://www.norwalkmusic.com
A superb online discount musical-instrument store with masses of links direct to manufacturers' websites, plus an index covering every instrument. Reasonably priced too.

Pignose http://www.pignoseamps.com
Legendary amplifiers for almost 25 years. Plug in, turn up to 12, start up and, as the mighty Lemmy put it, watch your neighbour's lawn die.

Proaudio.Net http://www.proaudio.net
Equipment and production from a firm almost as direct and classy as their name.

Roland   http://www.edirol.co.uk

Roland have a reputation for keeping abreast of new technology. A must for lovers of keyboards and gadgets alike.

Starland   http://www.starland.co.uk

UK mail-order store for midi and other gear. Reasonably priced, and helpful for those moody artists who don't like to leave the house.

Technics   http://www.panasonic.com/consumer_electronics/
technics_audio

Shout going out to turntables and keyboards. For years the biggest name in DJ equipment.

Vestax   http://www.vestax.co.uk

Mixers, turntables and merchandise – dance music paradise.

Yamaha   http://yamaha.com

Yamaha equipment – usually cheap, sturdy, effective and easy to have repaired. Famous last words?

Information/News

1212   http://www.1212.com

With an average of 32,000 unique visitors every day, this is the most widely used resource for musicians worldwide. Although the database is far from definitive, it covers most of the ground from legal aid to songwriting.

Independent Records   http://www.indierec.com

All about bar codes. A useful site, honest.

Making Music   http://www.makingmusic.co.uk

The subscription magazine every professional musician reads in the loo now goes online to blow its own trumpet. Psst! Wanna buy a Fender Strat?

Music Dish http://www.musicdish.com
Includes industry news and jobs. there are also tips for ruthless self-promotion at http://www.musicdish.com/main/tips_top.html.

Music Search http://www.musicsearch.com
A good one-stop for musician info. Stop by for a casual browse – you will definitely learn something.

The Music Week News http://www.dotmusic.com/news
Updated daily. A tad dull for outsiders but, for industry types, it's a buzzing hive of intrigue. Try reading between the lines.

Musicians Atlas http://musiciansatlas.com
A useful guidebook for working musicians.

NME http://www.nme.com
Up-to-date news, and you can leave your demo in the A&R section. And wait for your calls to be returned.

The Tip Sheet http://www.tipsheet.co.uk
Jonathan King's industry mag – without buying a subscription, find out what the pluggers are plugging and why the execs are whingeing, and get sound clips, a forum for bigwigs and a 'Crystal Ball' feature.

The Velvet Rope http://www.velvetrope.com
A US music-industry subscription site – gossip about people you've never heard of.

Legal

The Copyright Website http://www.benedict.com
Practical copyright information. For those who like to know what they're signing. Babies and habitual victims need not apply.

Department of Culture, Media and Sport   http://www.culture.gov.uk

Some British bands do enjoy Lottery awards. So go on, try it on. Is there any reason why you couldn't be an important cultural ambassador for your nation? No, thought not. Also at http://www.lottery.culture.gov.uk.

The Simpkins Partnership   http://www.simpkins.com/practice/music.htm

Large firm of entertainment lawyers offer advice. Hmm, sounds dodgy. But they do actually offer you more than just a terse 'Hands up'.

World Intellectual Property Organisation   http://www.wipo.org

Highbrow song-rights site. Remember, MP3 can be both a boon and a bane to the songwriter, and there are any number of advertisers (and other songwriters!) willing to 'borrow' from your oeuvre. It's a good idea to find out where you stand.

Live Gigs

What follows is a small selection of London venues, just as a taster and a guide to what might be available to you as a gigging band or solo musician. You'll also find plenty of addresses by making use of the search engines and portals listed in Chapter 3 and the magazines in Chapter 4. For US venues, we heartily recommend Rolling Stone at http://www.rollingstone.tunes.com/sections/localmusic, where you'll find a weekly round-up of rock shows to see, plus details of all the venues involved.

The Borderline   http://www.borderline.co.uk

A useful what's-on guide to one of London's premier venues based just over the road from Denmark Street, better known as Tin Pan Alley.

Bull & Gate   http://www.bullandgate.co.uk
One of the best and most influential small venues in London
produces a content-stuffed site.

Jazz Cafe   http://www.jazzcafe.co.uk/index2.htm
Flash site for great Camden venue.

Mean Fiddler   http://www.meanfiddler.com
Get your demos off there now.

Music And Gigs Link   http://www.musiciansgiglink.com
Gigs and contacts.

The New   http://www.
Acoustic Movement   windbob.demon.co.uk
Acoustic music showcases and clubs in London and the UK.

The Original Songwriters   http://www.
Showcase   showcaselondon.co.uk
London's longest-running weekly live songwriter showcase.

Managers

*You may feel that you can give full rein to your creative nature and
stay on top of business at the same time. Most can't. The business
side can be massively time-consuming, and also so frustrating,
sickening and cruel that it may not leave you in a fit mood to write
songs. Having to 'work' the sprawling Internet doesn't make it
easier. Sounds like you need someone on your side.*

Association of Independent Music   http://www.musicindie.com
Useful for finding a manager. And, make no mistake, finding a
good one is one of the most important things you'll ever do.

International Managers Forum.   http://www.imf-uk.org
Most good managers are members. Recommended.

Missmanagement   http://www.btinternet.com/
                                          ~missmanagement

Blade's manager sells her management skills with this garish website.

Worlds End Management   http://www.harbour.sfu.ca/
                                          ~hayward/van/van.html

US-based, so worth trying even for European outfits. Remember, if you haven't cracked America, you haven't cracked anything. And who better to help you?

Manufacturing

Unfortunately it's extremely dull but, as the digital revolution is not quite upon us, still extremely necessary.

Cops   http://www.cops.co.uk/cops

Music and software manufacturing in the UK. Plus jokes.

Distronics   http://www.disctronics.co.uk

Manufacturing in the UK, Europe and USA.

Disc Makers   http://www.discmakers.com

The number-one manufacturer for the US independent-music industry.

MP3

There are many more MP3 sites in Chapter 7 which will help you to track down almost any MP3 file your heart could desire. The following are specifically for new, unsigned artists.

Audio Galaxy   http://www.audiogalaxy.com

With an impressive amount of traffic, 25 megabytes of space on their server for each artist, reviews and very few bugs, this comes highly recommended.

CDIY   http://www.cdiy.com

'Welcome to the future of music', they brag, but actually this custom CD/MP3 site is brimming with interesting new talent selected by a crack editorial team. The only drawback is that the text is so small you need a microscope to decipher it.

Changemusic   http://www.changemusic.com

The animation that starts this site is amusing and the consequent uploading/turnaround short and sweet. You can check your stats as well.

Garageband   http://www.garageband.com

Before you can post your stuff, you have to listen to and vote for ten tracks already on the site. This takes a while but is fun, and the quality is surprisingly good. Which bodes well for traffic here.

Listen   http://www.listen.com

Calling itself a Music Download Directory, this is simple and it's quick to sign up. They give your music a fair text description, plus postings for musicians who are looking for film music work.

mp3.com   http://www.mp3.com

Mentioned elsewhere in this book, but worth noting again here, this is the unsigned-band MP3 site that musicians recommend – well laid out, interesting (if you have your own MP3s, it is impossible not to become obsessed with the statistics) and by far the most traffic of all MP3 sites.

Music Builder   http://www.MusicBuilder.com

Recommended, quick to sign up and upload and there's a good feel. You can check your statistics whenever you want to as well.

Nusounds   http://www.nusounds.com

As well as hosting MP3s they will include a photo, biog, song description and contact information. Easy and quick to sign up to.

Rolling Stone
http://www.rollingstone.com

Blimey, even the big boys are at it – then again, Rolling Stone has such a brilliant site it could fit into pretty much any address book in this guide. With their MP3 section, it's easy to get your material uploaded and the biog details in, but the company you will keep in the fortnightly chart is off-putting if you have ideas about being cutting-edge.

The Ultimate Band List
http://www.ubl.com

Again, mentioned elsewhere here for its utter brilliance in other areas, the UBL, one of the longest running music sites, will also host your MP3s. You currently get 10 megabytes of space plus a biog, pictures and links.

Yahoo Digital
http://digital.broadcast.com/digital/audio

You don't get more than one song, a picture and a biog, but the sign-up is simple and the uploading time short.

Official Bodies

For all its historic lawlessness, rock 'n' roll has its rules, and they are rules many are prepared to break for financial gain and often to your personal detriment. Here's a list of potential friends in your ongoing struggle to get what's coming to you.

ASCAP
http://www.ascap.com

Largest US collection agency (they're the ones who ensure that radio stations, TV companies, supermarkets *et al.* pay up for using your material) and allegedly the most often visited professional music website.

The British Phonographic Industry
http://www.bpi.co.uk

All about the Brits, plus careers in the industry, statistics and links. Recommended.

Incorporated Society of Musicians   http://www.ism.org
More classical than pop, but still worth a peek if you're at all
interested in self-preservation.

Independent Musicians Guild   http://www.scimg.com/img
A useful guide for anyone who'd like to be hard and cool and
take no shit from anyone, but actually works better as part of a
big gang.

MCPS   http://www.mcps.co.uk
In alliance with the PRS, the Mechanical Copyright Protection
Society are one of the largest collection agencies in the world,
working on behalf of songwriters and artists.

Musicians' Union   http://www.musiciansunion.org.uk
A simple but very useful site designed for both those new to it all
and those sporting mullets.

NUS   http://www.nus.org.uk
Students' Union website – useful contacts and a gig guide.

PRS (Performing Right Society)   http://www.prs.co.uk
The UK association of composers, songwriters and music
publishers. It administers the 'performance right' in their music.

Producers

---

*In Chapter 8, you'll find a selection of sites dedicated to the
world's hottest and heaviest record producers. Below is a list of
sites that should prove enormously helpful to anyone looking for
technical assistance in recording their music – from those with not
a penny to those with an absurdly inflated major label budget.*

The Encyclopaedia of   http://www.
Record Producers   mojavemusic.com
A massive database of producers. You should find something here.

Helium http://www.helium.co.uk
UK management for Tears For Fears, plus Tori Amos producers Ian
Stanley, Chris Hughes and others.

Music Producers Guild http://www.mpg.org.uk
Of good use to pros. Get the relevant info direct from the horse's
mouth.

Music Producers Guild Of America http://www.mpga.org
Don't expect Phil Spector to be a member.

PB Management http://www.pbmanagement.co.uk
News, sound clips and discographies on the producers of the
Stereophonics, Elastica etc.

Re-Pro International http://www.aprs.co.uk
A very useful resource for producers, engineers and anyone serious
about recording music. For the rest of us, perhaps a little on the
wrist-slashingly dull side.

SJP Productions http://www.sjpdodgy.co.uk/main.html
Really interesting; they look after producers who work or have
worked with Pink Floyd, Radiohead, Mansun and Tricky.

Stephen Budd Management http://www.record-producers.com/
Check out the management for, among others, the producer of
Travis and the Manics.

Publishing

*Ever wondered how bands got their music used on adverts or
in the latest smash from Leonardo Di Caprio? The following are
the guys that organise all that stuff – for a more than modest
percentage, it must be said. But everyone still wants a publishing
deal. If you're a songwriter, it's where you'll find the big advance*

fees – which you don't have to pay back even if you don't sell a single album.

Capricorn   http://www.capricornmusic.com
Dutch independent music publishing company searching for all genres of commercial music from across the globe.

EMI Music Publishing   http://www.emimusicpub.com
More for business clients than for aspiring bands, sadly.

The Franchesa Group   http://www.franchesa.com
Represents writers from around the world and licenses music.

Global Music Group   http://www.globalmusicgroup.de
An international publishing giant, with operations in Germany, the UK and the USA.

Mean Fiddler   http://www.mean-fiddler-
Music   music.co.uk/look.htm
Linked with Warner Chappell and looking for new writers.

Music Publishers Association   http://www.mpa.org
Loads of FAQs for budding songwriters.

The Parker Music Group   http://www.musicclearance.com
Credits include Titanic, Ally McBeal and The X Files – find out about selling your tunes.

Peermusic   http://www.peermusic.com
One of the world's largest independent music companies.

Warner Chappell   http://www.warnerchappell.com
US site for the international publisher. Very big, very rich. They like to keep their advances up over £100,000 – so try to be exceptionally talented if you can.

Recording Studios

Bear in mind that any studio putting up a website may well be a little more upmarket than some standard demo studios. However, even the big London studio websites are worth visiting, if only to see what you have to look forward to when you have a record deal. For many more US studio sites, many of the US magazines mentioned in Chapter 4 run helpful sections. We once again recommend Rolling Stone.

Air   http://www.airstudios.com
A Real Audio stream of George Martin's voice. Worth a visit, but don't think about doing your demos here.

Battery   http://www.battery-studios.co.uk
London-based, mid-range prices.

Blackwing   http://www.blackwing.co.uk/Studios/Index.html
London-based, good-value indie studio.

Brill Building   http://www.brillbuilding.pair.com
Not the New York workplace of Neil Sedaka, Neil Diamond and Carole King, but a cool if relatively down-at-heel Glasgow studio.

Chipping Norton   http://www.cnrs.clara.net
Great residential in the Cotswolds with fab in-house engineer.

Courtyard   http://www.barris.u-net.com/court1.htm
Radiohead and Supergrass's management run this reasonably priced residential.

Eden   http://www.edenstudios.com
London-based and pricey.

Fairview   http://www.fairview-music.demon.co.uk
In Hull. Then again, so for a long time was Norman Cook (back when he was a Housemartin and not a Fatboy).

Hear No Evil   http://hearnoevil.net
Fair price, and nothing whatsoever to do with Twisted Sister.

Jacobs   http://www.jacobs-studios.co.uk
Reasonably priced Surrey-based residential with swimming pool. If you fancy making a bit of a splash, like.

Le Mons   http://www.le-mons.co.uk
The most fashionable place on Earth – South Wales – offers a bargain studio.

Mayfair   http://www.mayfair-studios.co.uk
Primrose Hill's finest – Spice Girls to Travis record here, so dress for success.

Metropolis   http://www.demon.co.uk/
                                    studiobase/metro/index.html
Renowned for the mastering capabilities of Tim Young, this is a London Bond-movie-set of a studio. Ah, so we finally meet ...

Milo   http://www.demon.co.uk/studiobase/milo/index.html
London-based. Good value, for any musician feeling the pinch (about 99.999 per cent of you).

Nomis   http://www.nomis-net.com
Pricey, spacious, full of famous people and close to Olympia, in case you're partial to enormous cultural events like the Boat Show. You can rehearse here too.

Odessa   http://surf.to/odessa
Worth a visit. It's a lot more welcoming than the name suggests.

Panther http://ds.dial.pipex.com/sema/panther.htm

London – small and cosy. Should perhaps be named Koala.

Park Lane http://www.pls.uk.com

Glasgow-based and quality. Well regarded by a Scottish scene that's remarkably consistent in its busyness.

Parr St http://www.merseyworld.com/parr

Great studio in Liverpool. Visit the Cavern in your hours off and dream of future glory.

RAK http://www.rakstudios.co.uk

All the greats, from Suzi Quatro to Radiohead, have recorded here in St John's Wood – and it's still brilliant.

Rich Bitch http://www.rich-bitch.co.uk

Reliable rooms in Birmingham. Slade worked here, as, much later, did the Charlatans.

Ridge Farm http://www.ridgefarmstudio.com

Oasis recorded 'Be Here Now' here. But you could make a better go of it.

Rockfield http://www.demon.co.uk/
studiobase/rockfield/index.html

Welsh titan of a studio, situated just outside Monmouth. 'Bohemian Rhapsody' was recorded here – check out the pix.

Sawmills http://www.sawmills.co.uk

Good-value Cornish residential, out in the middle of absolutely nowhere. Excellent for those who find it hard to concentrate when surrounded by that urban kerfuffle. Supergrass record here.

September Sound http://www.ctnet.demon.co.uk/sept

Cocteau Twins' studio, so perfect if you want your CD to sound as if it fell from heaven. You might need to hire Robin Guthrie as producer, though.

The Stables   http://www.stables-studio.demon.co.uk
A good reason to go to Lincolnshire. Sometimes sausages are just not enough.

Trident   http://www.trident-net.com
A bargain, and so near New Scotland Yard – handy if thieves make off with your equipment, or your drummer.

Wool Hall   http://www.sonicstate.com/woolhall
Van Morrison's studio near Bath. Excellent facilities in one of England's most beautiful cities. Just don't drink the water – it's warm. Yuck.

Songwriters

If you ever thought you were out there on your own, mis-understood and doomed to forge your writing craft alone in a freezing garret, you'll be amazed by how many sites there are dedicated to songwriters. You'll find business advice, tips on honing your skills, and a lot of friendly people who were or are in the same boat as you. There's a lot of money in publishing, and these sites will help you get your share.

American Songwriter   http://www.americansongwriter.com
Lots of news and tips for those aspiring. An important site.

British Academy of   http://www.
Composers and Songwriters   britishacademy.co.uk
A single voice for UK music writers, and a great place to find people who are on your side.

Lyrics Review   http://www.lyricsreview.com
Submit lyrics for review. But don't be precious, they will be reviewed.

Muse's Muse   http://www.musesmuse.com/
Great site for songwriters. Everything you need to know business-wise, plus creative tips.

Music And Lyrics   http://www.music-and-lyrics.co.uk
Songwriting tips, if you fancy going beyond 'Gonna write a classic, gonna write it in an attic'.

Online Rhyming   http://www.link.cs.cmu.edu/
Dictionary   rhyme-doc.html
I know a girl called Elsa, she's into Alka Seltzer. Hmm, must try harder.

Songlink   http://www.songlink.com
Premiere site for serious songwriters. 40,000 men and women every day, 40,000 ... (well, maybe not that serious).

Songwriters   http://www.freeyellow.com/
Haven   members5/jamielc/index.html
Don't give up, as Pete Gabriel and Kate Bush begged us all those years ago.

Thesaurus   http://www.link.cs.cmu.edu/lexfn
Enormously helpful if you can't quite find the perfect word to describe just how much they hurt you.

Webster's Dictionary   http://www.m-w.com/dictionary.htm
Goodbye paper, hello shelf space. More words than you could ever possibly need, even if you do intend to put out as many albums as Frank Zappa.

Training

A career in music is now taken a great deal more seriously by both government and educational establishments. Grants are available to some, and there are thousands of courses available. Remember, it's not all about being the lead singer, bathed in limelight. You could play any number of instruments in any number of styles. You could be a producer, a mixer, an engineer. You could be a manager, an agent, a promoter. You could work in sleeve design, press, manufacturing or distribution. The following should help to widen your options.

Association of Professional   http://www.
Recording Services   aprs.co.uk
Search for education and training, or become a member.

The Brit School   http://www.brit.croydon.sch.uk
Officially sanctioned music-biz school. Intended to be the British equivalent of that crazy academy in Fame.

Musebiz.Com   http://www.musebiz.com
For music-biz education. Easily navigable and a fair eye-opener for beginners.

Musicianswalk   http://www.musicianswalk.com/page2.html
Guitar lessons and acoustic news. A friendly and helpful approach.

The National Centre for   http://www.
Popular Music   ncpm.co.uk
Learn about the music biz. The NCPM is Sheffield-based but still regarded as the jewel in the UK's musical crown.

Reach For the Sky   http://www.sky.co.uk/RFTS/index2.htm
Millennial advice on making it for teenagers.

Recording Connection   http://www.recordingconnection.com
Learn to be an engineer. Then you can rise to the status of producer. Then you can command fees and percentage points that would make the US President sick with jealousy.

Songplayer   http://www.songplayer.com
Super-fast tuition for guitar and keyboards. Try both at the same time. You may never have a hit, but a bright future in the circus is guaranteed.

UK Regional

Irish Music Rights Organisation   http://www.imro.ie
U2, the Corrs, Clannad, Van Morrison – here's plenty of advice for those wishing to find a place in that hallowed pantheon.

New Music In Scotland   http://www.nemis.co.uk/2main.htm
Help for Scottish artists. Come on, brave hearts, let's see what you're made of.

South East England   http://dialspace.dial.
Music Alliance   pipex.com/sema
A site that's dedicated to independent and underground music in London and the southeast of England. Try it. We all need someone we can lean on.

10//THE FUTURE NOW?

Digital downloading and the casual passer-by

In this book, we've considered the ways in which the Internet has already changed the music industry – the way music is marketed and sold, the way it's presented and even recorded. Plans are afoot, though, to change things still further.

Naturally, the big companies are involved, testing the ground for their latest sales ideas. One of these is Musicmaker, whose operation was described in Chapter 1, and one of their ideas was a kiosk where you could download the music of your choice and have it printed on a personalised CD while you wait.

Tests have already been carried out, with 25 such kiosks being placed in 20 US cities. The kiosks themselves are 24-by-30-foot (6-by-9-metre), stand-alone units with touch-screen monitors. They have on-screen animation and voice direction to lead customers through each step of the process. You get to choose tracks from Musicmaker's file – which at the time of testing numbered 200,000 but will soon approach the million mark – and can 'preview' any of them before you seal the deal.

The first five tracks will set you back $9.95 (compared with the $4.95 you pay if you do it from home – though the kiosk charges no postage on top), then it's $1 for each additional track. You get to add your own CD title and a graphic for the label. The kiosk accepts both cash and credit cards, and will drop your CD into your hands in five minutes or less, including a jewel case and a tray card listing the tracks you've chosen. You don't have to download on to CD, either. You can also record direct on to your portable player. The initial kiosks supported the download of secure MP3 files straight into Diamond Multimedia's Rio 500.

And, thankfully, it's not all just about selling. Or at least some clear-cut cultural good is being done. The plan, in the United States at first, is also to set up these kiosks in museums, where visitors will be able to compile CDs from 32,000 tracks of historic US music from the Smithsonian/Folkways Collections. It's a notion that could be of tremendous benefit to archivers of music everywhere, as well as to canny sample fiends like Moby.

Shop to live, live to shop?
One can only assume that the boom created in the music market by the Internet will turn nasty for some. There are too many sites setting themselves up as mega-markets. It would be a miracle if none of them were overextending themselves and doomed to crash and burn. In the meantime, consumers can expect to see the best of all possible worlds as competition for market share drives down the prices charged by the giant retailers, while at the same time forcing them to increase their range and improve their services. Small, specialist retailers should survive and bloom, as storing albums digitally means they can meet demand without having to risk sinking all their cash into stock that might sit in the racks for years.

It does seem that traditional music retailing may become a thing of the past. Perhaps the big chains will attempt to take over retailing on the Net. It's hard to believe that they could keep their expensive high-street shop spaces without adapting to what will almost certainly be a dramatic drop in sales. They may well turn themselves into Internet shopping centres, with comfortable furnishings and a funky atmosphere. Many have already experimented with ideas similar to Musicmaker's kiosk. Perhaps the two might go together, with a communal gathering of individuals, each wearing headphones and lost in music. Cool, eh?

Others foresee tremendous advances in digital downloading with music providers becoming ever more sensitive to the tastes and desires of the customer, and the customer demanding absolute simplicity. Jo Sager, vice-president of Tunes.com, pictured a time when we would pay '$10 a month for a download subscription'. Every night we'd place our player in its cradle and it would download the ten new songs of the day. The website providing the music would discuss our likes with the player, and all the obvious no-noes would be cut out automatically, leaving us to choose from an agreeably manageable list.

Many would have us believe that the arrival of a better infrastructure in the form of cable modems, DSL and ADSL (see Chapter 7) will make digital downloading so fast and convenient that high-street stores will be killed outright, and that the CD format will perish along with them. Others claim that the enjoyment of music is to a great degree a shared experience and consequently ill-suited to a housebound existence. Some will tell you that DSL will matter not a jot as downloading via radio waves is the Next Big Thing (sorry for recommending all that equipment if it is).

Record companies: back in the saddle?
One thing's for dead certain. Whatever happens, the major labels (of which there are now really only four) will not let go of the reins of production and distribution without a scrap. They have clearly been threatened by the MP3 format and, unable to encode a secure and customer-friendly alternative, have begun to fight back, tooth and nail.

At the time of writing, ten major members of the RIAA are suing the powerful MP3.com to the tune of billions. The problem is this: with their Beam-It and Instant Listening Service, MP3.com were allowing their members to purchase music from an online retailer and also, by placing CDs they already owned in their CD-ROM drive and 'beaming' them instantly to MP3.com, they would be able to listen to those CDs wherever they were – the service being described as 'a virtual CD player'. You could thus theoretically access your entire music collection from any computer with a web connection.

The record companies disapprove heartily. Though MP3.com claim, quite rightly, that users must necessarily have purchased any CD they were accessing, the companies reckon MP3.com have copied 45,000 albums, with no permission and no licence, for their own commercial gain. They're thus behaving like a radio station, but paying no fees or royalties. MP3.com have sworn to fight to the bitter end. And, really, it can only be bitter. You can keep up with this case, and all the others that will doubtless follow, by visiting the news sections and archives at ASCAP (**http://www.ascap.com**), Rolling Stone (**http://www/rollingstone.com**) and MP3.com themselves (**http://www.mp3.com**), and the MP3 pages at the worthy and ever-informative About.com (**http://www.about.com**).

The secure sale of music and the prevention of web thievery is a major headache for the companies. All manner of possibilities have been put forward. Music sites may be able to track down people who download without paying, but they can't stop people buying CDs and uploading them for others to download, not if it's done quickly and through cowboy newsgroups. They say they could invent digital music players that won't play music unless its sale was authorised, even players so hyper-secure they would email the authorities if you tried to play an unauthorised file. But they're not here yet. And, if a secure system was invented (and it's generally claimed that one already has been), how could it be popularised with so many companies pushing so many different digital audio players, all of them fighting tooth and nail for a bigger market share. After all, the public are interested in convenience, sound quality and their favourite artists, not how much the record companies are making. And really it's only the public's decency that's keeping piracy at bay.

It's the Wild West out there. Thrilling. Yes, yes, but what's it got to do with me?

There are many music fans who feel they'd like things to stay pretty much as they are. They like to go rooting for new or old musical delights in racks of vinyl or CDs; they like to be in attendance when their favourite acts are in town, every two or three years or so. There's a sense of familiarity and comfort to it all.

The Internet will not necessarily change any of it. The amount of music bought online will certainly increase as prices are lower, and downloading or delivery makes the experience extremely convenient for the consumer. But record shops will adapt and probably survive, particularly shops specialising in particular genres. These are often run by obsessives who like to spend their days surrounded by their stock – a stock that in their case is more of a glorified record collection – and who love to meet their customers. The Internet, with its chat rooms and bulletin boards and fan clubs and societies, can improve your social life, but there's only so far it can take you.

Then there are live shows broadcast over the web. We've already witnessed large-scale festival-style events such as NetAid, where performances by the likes of George Michael and Sheryl Crow could be viewed simultaneously by hundreds of millions of people, and this trend will doubtless continue. Before the Internet, such a massive audience could be achieved only via a complex bargaining process involving TV companies in hundreds of different countries. Only very special events could justify the effort and the expense – Live Aid, the Oscars maybe, or the Superbowl. Now, if you're any kind of musician, it could be you.

Live Webcasts are already commonplace on the web. They take place every day, and this guide has already shown you where to find them. It makes sense that more and more bands will reach out to the public in this way, for many reasons. For a start, many musicians hate to play before a live audience – stage fright, controlling nature, you name it – and plenty hate the rigours of touring. Webcasts allow them to play to all their fans, all at once, from the musician's own front room, if they like. Hey, you could even record a show over a period of months, perfecting every aspect, and then broadcast it to everyone. And think of bands who have just a handful of fans in each town. Rather than play every toilet in Christendom and beyond, losing their dignity, their minds and all their money as they go, they can play to all of them at the same time.

Gigs, of course, can make money. Bands can gross millions, and some survive for years on the proceeds from T-shirt sales at gigs. But webcasts can be pay-per-view, and fans need click just once to go to a virtual merchandise stall far better stocked than any real one could be. And, besides, for most acts gigs are not big earners, just a way to promote the product that does turn a profit – the album. With the Internet, you can promote that hard, all the way through the gig.

Of course, there will still be tours. Many musicians still consider this to be their only means of genuinely communicating with their audience. They see gigs as an emotional give and take between themselves and the crowd, with the performers reacting to the general mood and often being driven on to greater creative peaks. They love the travel, the camaraderie and the concomitant shenanigans. And this is not to mention ego and the burning desire many performers have to be up there in front of the world, right at the centre of what Albert Speer called a 'cathedral of light'.

As members of the audience, we love it too. We love to be in the presence of our idols, love to be swept along by the mood and movement of the crowd. For us, gigs are social events and, though we might be able to save a webcast for posterity, they surely won't contain any of the personal moments that make gigs so special. They'll capture the stage show and the performance, but not the part when your best friend threw up on the security guard, or when you bumped into Trent Reznor in the queue for hot dogs (he's human too).

What the Internet offers is more, more of everything. If you can't get tickets, you can still attend a show. If a band's on tour, and is really on the ball webwise, you might be able to attend all the shows, without any of the hassle and expense you'd usually have to suffer (though, for many, that's part of the fun). You can conveniently watch shows you'd never normally go to, thus widening your experience, and maybe finding new bands and genres to explore. And there's also the chance that big gigs could become major social events. Just as we all tuned in to see the TV launch of Madonna's 'Like a Prayer' video, or the final episode of Seinfeld, or the Tyson-Holyfield fights, so Internet concerts might become the day's big talking point, worldwide. What if that happened and the lead singer started talking about the CIA selling drugs in US ghettos? We're back to the 60s – music as revolution.

Slicing the pie: is there any left?

Perhaps the last word should be left to the conspiracy theorists. It's already being whispered that the freedom granted by the Internet is to be short-lived, that the enormous corporate groups now being formed – in particular the AOL-Time-Warner-EMI group – are soon to take over entirely. By buying up the artists, the labels, the retailers, the servers, the search engines, everything, they can ensure that only their products are made, marketed and sold.

Maybe there's some truth in there. The eventual reassertion of the status quo is not a shocking idea (as long as it doesn't entail the reassertion of Status Quo). But, at the moment, it does seem that the Internet cannot be tamed. Insiders are likening it to the Wild West for good reason. Like the best music, it retains its fiercely independent spirit, and for that it should be applauded.

The arrival of the Internet has made a dreadful mess of music. No one can be quite sure where it's all headed. Creativity is being called for and, as this guide proves, the call is being answered. There can be no doubt that these are the most fascinating of times.

So, come on. Bring the noise ...

//INDEX

//NOTES

CLICKMUSIC.co.uk

//SIMPLY SEARCHING FOR MUSIC

With millions of websites dedicated to music on the net, **Clickmusic. co.uk** makes sense of the noise by sorting the good from the bad. It is the definitive gateway to the best music on the web.

Clickmusic.co.uk has the first independent search engine focused exclusively on searching for UK music on the web - from record companies promoting new bands, retailers selling CDs and MP3 sites for music downloads to fan sites, music news, reviews and online tickets.

//MP3s

As more and more artists are using the Internet to offer exclusive downloadable tracks to fans, Radio One's Steve Lamacq has been recruited to Clickmusic.co.uk to cast an authoritative ear over the best tracks available wherever they are online. There's even the world's first ever Top Ten MP3 Chart, based on user's votes.

//MUSIC NEWS

Music News on Clickmusic.co.uk is updated every five minutes from over 30 sources, 24 hours a day, 365 days a year - making sure that you get all the news as it happens.

//SHOPBOT™

If you're buying CDs online, the **Clickmusic.co.uk** ShopBot brings you the largest selection of online music retailers in one place and searches through all the major online retailers for great prices. Even the more obscure purchases are available through **Clickmusic. co.uk**, including sheet music, hi-fi, MP3 players and even guitars.

//CSPOT™

CSpot's dedicated student area is fast becoming a major meeting point for students who are into music, and is devoted to championing new musical talent on the web. CSpot is the source for discovering new signed music online, including in-depth interviews, news, reviews and the inevitable competitions. Oh, and there's education and jobs too - but only if you want to get into the music business.

//BAND GUIDE

With over 2,000 artists in the Clickmusic band guide, you're only ever one click away from the best of everything online for your favourite artist. Be it their official website, the most crazed fan site, the latest news or album reviews and tours, you'll find it all here.

//PLAYROOM

It's not all serious! In the Clickmusic.co.uk Playroom, you'll find brilliant music based games online - including the legendary No.1 Game that casts a wry look at the ugly underbelly of the music industry, allowing players to guide their own careers through a minefield of choices to try and top the charts.

//CLICK CLUB

Register for the Click Club and get the star treatment – receive exclusive tailored music information, online discounts, privileged access to clubs and gigs and even free music and other goodies.

Also published in the Virgin Internet Guide series...

The Virgin Guide to the Internet
The advice you need to plug in, log on and get going.

The Virgin Family Internet Guide
The only book that lets your family get the best out of the Internet
– and lock out the worst.

The Virgin Internet Shopping Guide
You can now buy almost anything on the Internet, and this book
shows you how.

The Virgin Internet Travel Guide
The complete guide to choosing your destination
– and getting the best deal online.

The Virgin Internet Money Guide
Get your personal finances sorted – online.

Forthcoming titles:

The Virgin Internet Business Guide
The essential companion for anyone in business.

The Virgin Internet Research Guide
How to find out just about anything on the net

The Virgin Weird Internet Guide
Strange and wonderful places to surf.

The Virgin Internet Auction Guide
Bid for a bargain.

For more information, ask your friendly local bookseller – or check
out our website: **http://www.virgin-books.com**